# Endorsements

*Dan Seaborn – Author, National Speaker, Founder of Winning at Home Inc., Featured Speaker at University Campuses and Church Events:*

"Mike is a man who has been thru it and can give all glory to God for learning to forgive by the grace of Christ. It's gritty and it's real. And it reflects how raw life can be! But if we seek God we will make it!"

*Gregg D. Glutting – National Chi Alpha Campus Ministries, Field Resource, Support Coach and Training Specialist:*

"If you've experienced trauma, if you or someone you know has struggled with forgiveness, this book is for you. Mike shares a traumatic event from his life, talks about its impact and shares his journey of forgiveness. His "Points to Ponder" will help you unlock your story to bring hope, forgiveness and freedom."

*Greg and Leah Molchan – Executive Directors of the Grand Rapids Dream Center:*

"I love the simplicity. I felt Mike taking a complex subject and making it simple to reflect on. I liked the realness of who Mike is and his story and how his experience comes through…it caused me to go back into similar situations and relate to it… other truths through your experience went into my heart but by the end of the book going into current hardness to embrace my own forgiveness journey. I have developed a daily practice of going back and forgiving those reoccurring thoughts. I loved how you kept Christ central…other people may have a different perspective but I'm a believer and it's true to who you are."

Love Jesus

*The*
POWER *of*
FORGIVENESS

Jan. 29. 11

# *The* POWER *of* FORGIVENESS

## The Key To Ultimate Freedom

## Michael Cooley Sr.

XULON PRESS

Xulon Press
2301 Lucien Way #415
Maitland, FL 32751
407.339.4217
www.xulonpress.com

Edited by Xulon Press

Printed in the United States of America.

ISBN-13: 978-1-54561-051-0

To the King of Kings and the Lord of Lords
Jesus Christ my Lord and Savior


This book is dedicated to my wife Robin. Our life
has grown together through loving and serving one
another. You have stood by my side as my biggest sup-
porter, best friend, and my partner in ministry. Thank
you for everything you are and everything you do. I am
thankful we serve a loving Father together.


For our wonderful family:

Mandy and Kenn, Isaiah and Zack
Michael and Brittany and Kaemin
Doug and Erin
Matthew and Victoria and Willem

# Contents

# Acknowledgments

Special thank you to:

Robin for her encouragement

Bob VandePol for his knowledge and encouragement

Charlotte Wilmore for her project management and editing support

Erin Glutting for her editing

Jami Winstrom for final editing expertise

A special thank you to the book review team: Duane Vander Klok, Mike Benson, Gregg Glutting, Doug Payne, Dan Seaborn, and Greg Molchan. Thank you for your ideas and suggestions to make this writing possible.

This book is my story from near tragedy to overcoming the past. The works of this book are a collaborative effort from my team; their assistance made the writing process possible.

My hope is that each reader examines their life, can cast away the pain and hurts of their past, find forgiveness in every area of their lives, and live each day in relationship with God the Father, Jesus the Son, and the Holy Spirit.

# Foreword

In my own life as a believer and throughout thirty-five years of pastoral ministry, I can think of no other single act a person can do that can bring greater joy, peace, and freedom than the act of forgiveness. Conversely, I can think of no other single act that can bring a lifetime of sorrow, bitterness, and regret than the act of unforgiveness.

As it's been said, unforgiveness is like keeping someone locked in a cage in your heart, periodically bringing them out and beating them up, then sticking them back inside.

The problem with unforgiveness is that it becomes a cage unto itself. We step inside our own cage and bitterness entraps our life.

As I read Mike's book I so appreciated how he shared his story. Even though traumatic, it's honest and real. He then relates his story to a vast number of hurts, offenses, and even heart-wrenching events others face in their life.

You may be one of those people. Have you experienced trauma, been victimized, or lived through a tragic event? Have those experiences cut your heart, wounded you? Do they continually drag you down? Do you relive them day after day, year after year? Does it seem daunting and hopeless, like you can't get away from the pain they caused inside? If so, there is hope. There is a path to escape within the pages of this book

Mike not only shares real experiences but he leads you to a place of personal reflection and insight. You'll find application questions and points to ponder that will help you see and understand your own life's events in ways you've not seen before.

My encouragement is to read this book and ask the Holy Spirit to shine his light into your heart. If you are wrestling through your own life's experience this book will encourage, enlighten, and equip you. You'll find strength and healing for the challenges you've faced.

I know Mike's heart is to share the freedom and the steps to freedom that he's found. My hope and prayer is that you'll open this book to find all that God has to offer you through the power of forgiveness.

*Gregg D. Glutting*

*National Chi Alpha Campus Ministries, Field Resource, Support Coach and Training Specialist*

# Introduction

Romans 8:37, NIV — "No, in all these things
we are more than conquerors through him
who loved us."

Writing this book, *The Power of Forgiveness*, is a for-
ty-two-year journey. My life has been full of many
interesting twists and turns. My story is a biographical
journey from a near-death tragedy as a teenager to living
a victorious life with a plan and purpose.

## Making Sense of My Life

It took years for me to understand who I was. After the
night of the robbery, everything changed for me. It's hard
for me to put into words what I was feeling, but something had changed. Years later as I reflected back, my
innocence was lost, or in reality, it was taken away from
me at the hands of common thieves.

What happened to me happens every day to others in
this world at the hands of robbers, abusers, and sexual
predators. Someone plans to take unfair advantage of the
innocent or people who are simply in the wrong place at
the wrong time. From the hard-working parents that get

the news a school bus carrying their children has been hit head-on by a drunk driver that's taken the life of their child, to a mother who goes to work her evening shift at the corner pharmacy when a robber points a gun in her face and demands the cash out of her register. Life changes from pleasant to frightening, being scared and following orders just to stay alive.

There are other examples: The unborn child who is innocently growing and developing safe inside the womb is fed a full dose of alcohol, cocaine, or other damaging drugs fueled by the mother's uncontrollable addiction to drugs and alcohol. An innocent child in development unable to fend off the toxic waste entering the developing baby's body through the umbilical cord.

The Bible says life is like a vapor; at any moment it can change or be over. With maturity comes knowledge and experience from life adventures. These times shape the person you have become. Either good, bad, or indifferent, what legacy will you leave behind? The hope of this writing is for you, the reader, to evaluate your life, make changes, to find forgiveness in your life, and to live in the freedom that Christ Jesus provides.

## Reconciling Past Mistakes

This book opens the door to forgiveness. The chapter "How Big Is Your God" explains the story of King David and all the sins and mistakes he made in his life. After reconciling his life with God, God said King David is a man after my heart. No matter what the reader has done in their lives, God offers forgiveness! God's forgiveness of our sins allows the reader to forgive others that have wronged them or hurt them. God knows everything, and one day we will meet Him face to face.

> Romans 14:11 (NLT) says, "…'As surely as I live', says the LORD, 'every knee will bend to me, and every tongue will confess and give praise to God.'"

## Understanding the Hurts and Abuse

The stories of hurts and abuse are different and unique to each individual: for some, extreme acts of violence against them as a child; to others, words spoken causing embarrassment in front of classmates or other bystanders. The severity of the abuses are all different and with a thousand different causes. However, Romans 8:39 (NLT) assures us, "…nothing in all creation will ever be able to separate us from the love of God that is revealed in Christ…"

## God Really Loves You

On your good days, on your less-than-good days, and days when you have had some failure, He loves you just the same. He removes your guilt and shame. Accept His love and move on from the past. He has removed it, and so should you.

How many times does God forgive you for the mistakes that you make over and over, the stuff that happens that nobody else knows? Your sins are removed as far as the east is from the west. And you cry out to God saying, "I'm sorry God, I'm sorry God." He responds by saying,

"My son, my daughter I love you, I love you." He calls you His own. He died for your sins, each and everyone one of them. Now you can live a life in freedom full of the promises He has given you.

## Giving My Life to Him

Growing up as a young child in my family, I knew and practiced the basics in my faith walk; a solid foundation was established. We prayed at the dinner table and bedtime. I can recall my mother reading her well-worn white-covered Bible that had ripped and folded pages.

My early childhood life, as I remember it, was changing as I drifted further away from our church foundation. I was living an all-for-me life, God was a million miles away, and it really didn't matter. Like most young people that relationship between me and God was for old people, or so I thought.

Life changes quickly sometimes: one second is the difference between the here and now and eternity. This book allows the reader to examine their own life and look deep into issues of hurt, pain, or abuse. For some being forgiven is an issue of the heart and cross; for others, it can be reconciling a wrong that they did to another person, a breach of trust, or being dishonest.

This book addresses the ability to forgive someone who has hurt you deeply, cheated on you, or abused you in a multitude of ways. Perhaps you were left alone or abandoned as a child, or you are the wife whose husband, tired of the routine responsibilities, walked out on his family, and left you for another.

Jesus died for you. He loves you so deeply; let Him take the heavy burden that you have been carrying for as long as you can remember. He is willing; He is here, He is able. Seek His love for your life and live in freedom from this moment on.

May your healing be complete in every area of your life. Live the life you were created to live. Walk forward living your life in confidence, living life intentionally, and on purpose.

# CHAPTER 1

# Walking Into Darkness

August 2009

> Deuteronomy 7:21, WEB —"You shall
> not be scared of them; for Yahweh your
> God is in the midst of you, a great and
> awesome God."

*The mental imprint that was left behind from
that horrible day is a reminder of the hurts,
trauma, and damage caused by others decades
before. Yet, God is my healer; through the power
of forgiveness, I am made well again.*

I left Grand Rapids early this August morning for Detroit,
Michigan to do a typical structural inspection of a now-
closed big-box retail building. There was nothing unusual
about today. I thought today's job would be just like all
the other evaluations I've conducted: looking for leaky
roofs, damaged walls, and general building conditions.

In Detroit, I met Rick (a retail manager) at a different
location to get the keys and begin the process. I followed

Rick to the closed building a few miles away. The drive up to the building wasn't unusual. There were various rival gang symbols on light poles and utility boxes in the neighborhood, seemingly typical in most inner city areas and common now in suburbs and even in small town America.

My building inspection today seemed no different from others I have done before on an empty building with some broken glass. The building was tagged from the neighborhood bullies trying to claim ownership of it or that particular city block. My thoughts wandered. *What gives you the right to claim this is yours with the spray painting and vandalism?*

Life on the street is simple: the meanest, most intimidating people win through violence, threats, and force greater than that of others. They inflict fear into those around them, causing everyday people to avoid them. That avoidance allows slow changes to take place, which finally gives way to thugs dominating city blocks or neighborhoods.

Being bad is like a kingship where the lesser gang members look up to the leader. He sets the plan, and others follow out his orders like servants, hoping to gain rank or favor within the gang. The gang members do not know any other way of life; they are simply a product of their toxic environment.

Some significant adult or maybe one of their parents is so negligent to the responsibility of adulthood or parenting that they only look to fulfilling their own need to get drunk or get high. Babies are born into a culture of addiction, neglect, and violence, suffering through unspeakable acts done in the home.

They witness their mothers being beaten, loved ones coming and going, sibling abuse, shootings, and a multitude of other types of violence. The structure of the family is exploded into a thousand pieces, and children's innocence is forever lost. This sets up a lifelong tone of hardened hearts. To the kids, it's an ordinary way of life. Often fending for themselves, kids grow up tough here.

With the need to use drugs and alcohol comes a life of crime so they can support their habit. Taking what is not yours becomes a part of normal everyday life. In all likelihood, the kids have not seen an adult holding down a job, let alone ever going to work themselves. So the inbred cycle of poverty and street gang behavior begins once again, continuing generation after generation, and with it comes the devaluing of every human life it encounters.

Most times I am escorted through the building as I inspect the structure, but not today. Rick unlocked the front door, and as we walked in he handed me a card with his telephone number and said, "Call me when you're done."

*Wait a minute...done...done what? I can hardly see in here. Where are the lights?* A coolness came over me like a chill as I glanced into the dimly lit building. There were just two lights on in the humongous one hundred-forty-thousand square foot building; all the others had been shot out or smashed by the homeless or vandals. Feeling nervous and scared as hell, I noticed every hair on my body was standing on end.

Rick reached for his keys and started to leave. He said, "I am locking you inside the building. Call me when you're done." In disbelief, I asked, "You are not walking through with me?" He replied with three or four swear words: "No, I am *not* going into the blankity-blank, blanking building; I'm *not* stepping one foot inside this building, and you're crazy to go in there!" With that, I was locked inside. I watched Rick walk across the parking lot to his sports car and drive away. I did not know Rick for more than a few minutes, but now that he left I was alone, really alone. Words cannot describe my feelings of fear as I turned and looked into the darkness and the wide open spaces of this once booming retail store.

> Exodus 20:20, NLT — "Don't be afraid,
> "Moses answered them, "for God has come
> in this way to test you, and so that your fear
> of him will keep you from sinning!"

How do you describe fear? It could be as mild as a knot in the pit of your stomach or as dramatic as sheer terror. I am a big man, six foot five inches tall, and weigh 265 pounds. Most people would quickly run from me rather than have any confrontation. I suspect fear is the number one weapon of gang-related activities as well. If they can intimidate you, they have already won. It is also the number one weapon of Satan himself. Fear can stop ordinary people in their tracks from trying something new, from stepping out of their comfort zone, or from doing anything at all. Fear can paralyze the strongest man or woman on the earth.

Some people have adult fears stemming out of their childhood. Perhaps the fears began in grade school when they were embarrassed in front of the class. The teacher called on them for the answer and they froze, noticing every eye was on them. The other kids started giggling, and the teacher asked the question again, thinking he/she was not heard correctly. Embarrassed this student sits there clueless, so the teacher calls on another who gives the easy answer. Quickly all eyes revert back to the first student for not knowing the easy answer. An experience like this would make it difficult later on for this adult to speak in public.

Or how about an unfortunate performance in Little League? Perhaps a young boy who is on first base receives the sign from the coach to steal second base. The boy nods to the coach in agreement and leads off the base. As the pitcher begins his windup, the boy leads off farther and then runs for all he's worth. Unexpectedly the catcher fires the ball to second base and the boy is tagged out by only four steps. His teammates roar with laughter as he's called out, stopping the late-inning rally. Dejected, he dusts himself off and with his head down he runs back to the bench. This boy might be held hostage by the fear or embarrassment of trying and failing in front of others, and later he may grow into a man who fears taking chances in life or business.

There are hundreds of times throughout life where we have stumbled and failed. Sometimes we can take responsibility for our actions, but other times we've been the victim of crimes, bullying, or abuse. Decades later these unprocessed or misinterpreted moments return like they happened yesterday. A moment of trauma can be tattooed in the layers of the brain, only to reveal itself thirty, forty or more years later in the form of some life-restricting lie or a promise to never let that painful event happen again.

The human brain is a complex thing. It's sometimes easy to forgive but almost impossible to forget.

Reaching for my phone, I called my wife Robin and asked her to pray for my safety. As I began to walk into the darkness, every bone in my body and every ounce of common sense said, *Run and get out of there as fast as you can! This is Detroit where they could care less about shooting me or hitting me in the head with a metal pipe. I am the outsider here moving into someone's personal space.*

> The mental imprint that was left behind is a reminder of the hurts, trauma, and damage caused by others decades before. God is my healer; through the power of forgiveness, I am made well again.

I can't describe the intensity of my fear. Every sense was on high alert as I turned and looked into the vast darkness that couldn't be overcome by the only two working lights in the center of the closed sales room. There was a struggle taking place within me. Part of me said, *Stop! Don't go another step,* while the other said, *This is your job; you're expected to do this.*

As I am not permitted to carry any weapons while on this customer's property, I move forward with a clipboard and a 4D cell Mag flashlight (like the ones the police carry while on patrol). Within the first thirty steps, I find where campfires have been used to cook food and provide warmth during brutally cold Michigan winter nights. Nothing fancy, just pieces of wood pallets or other scrap wood that would burn on what used to be the old retailer's sales floor.

Every step was creepy, to say the least. Each time my foot touched the ground, it was met with the sound of crushed and broken glass. No sneaking through this place; you could hear me coming from a mile away. Everywhere throughout the building were piles of human waste and a heavy smell of urine. It was amazing to the see the volume of broken liquor bottles covering the floor — every type and every brand. It seems homelessness, alcohol, and drug abuse go hand in hand.

Easily available the booze might fight off the thoughts of a life that could have been. Perhaps addiction is a way of dealing with personal fears and failures from a lifetime of difficult choices or being wronged by someone they trusted. Or simply a life gone wrong from bad circumstances and poor choices, resulting in a life of crime and dependency.

All too soon it was time to walk away from the lights and rely only on my flashlight for both light and personal protection, if needed. I would love to say I walked through the building step by step, carefully taking precarious notes, and documenting it all with pictures of the damaged structure. It was far from that. Every movement was hurried on account of the overwhelming nervousness I felt. Most people would have been scared out of their wits having to go around these blind corners. If someone was lurking in the darkness they surely would have heard and seen me coming well in advance.

I quickly made notes of roof leaks and broken dry wall. Next came the bathrooms, one of the most difficult things to do. I knew once I walked into the bathroom I could be blocked in or ambushed when I walked out. The other challenge was looking into the empty bathroom stalls.

Since the building's water was turned off, the toilets didn't flush; however, the homeless people and vandals still continued to use the toilets. So after years of vacancy each toilet stool was overflowing with human waste. This was a smelly, rotten, dirty place, and it made my lungs hurt from breathing the bad air. Words cannot describe how sick I felt after seeing this.

My inspection continued throughout offices and stock-rooms. I was always wondering if someone would be waiting outside an office door to hit me in the head with a chunk of cement or anything else that was handy. Nearing the end of the inspection, I was still nervous but was glad to be making it through without incident. I breathed a prayer, *Thank you, Lord, for protecting me and keeping me safe!* I eagerly reached for my phone and called Rick to let him know I was finished. Adding insult to injury, Rick didn't show up for a while, making me wait in the locked store for an hour and a half before returning to open the door for my release.

Putting as much distance between me and the dark-ness as possible, I stood inside what was once the store vestibule. Some of the glass doors and windows were smashed out and boarded up with plywood; others were still intact. As I waited to be let out, homeless people would creepily walk up, press their faces to the exterior glass (using their hands to shield the sun's glare), and look right at me. I suspect they wondered if I had left the building yet. I could hardly wait to get out of this place! Finally Rick drove up, unlocked the door, and let me out. No words were spoken. I was just relieved and happy to be safely out of there.

It was amazing to see the daylight and breathe the fresh air! What a sense of freedom I felt, just like walking out of prison. I was suddenly free from the fears and darkness, haunting crazy thoughts, and dangers that just minutes ago were as real to me as seeing this light of day. I immediately called my wife to tell her I was safe and out of danger. Once again I thanked the Lord for His protection.

Years have passed since that August day when I faced my fears by walking into a dark and dangerous building. I still sometimes wonder now just how crazy that was. I am sure most people would have been nervous and scared to take on such a feat. But for me the significance of the event was monumental: I just passed a valuable life test of facing my fears, pushing myself forward, and completing the task. I am thankful for having the strength to go back to a "place," a place where two brothers took away my innocence on a very hot August night thirty-eight years earlier. I could now stand tall in my new found confidence: it could be done. I did it and finished well!

## CHAPTER 1 DISCUSSION QUESTIONS

> ### LIFE LESSONS
>
> Through determination I fought through my fears walking into the dark abandoned retail store to do my inspection; at no time was I ever comfortable until I walked into the daylight toward my truck. To have successfully completed my task, considering my past experiences, I walked out believing I can do anything I set my mind to do. I am an overcomer.

## Points to Ponder

Is there an embarrassing childhood memory that you still reflect on today?

Have you ever done something like vandalism or stealing to fit into a group?

Have you ever used drugs or alcohol to help you feel better?

Have you ever been scared to do something based on past memories?

# CHAPTER 2

# Early Childhood

Romans 8:16, NLT—"For his Spirit joins with our spirit to affirm that we are God's children."

*To have grown up in a home where my parents truly loved and cared for each other set the tone and the foundation for my life.*

When I was a child I was free to act like a child. Childhood was a carefree time with no worries, no real demands, and none of the stresses of life. How blessed I was to grow up in a stable, loving home with parents who loved each other and guided their children toward adulthood. I was born the last of four children in the late nineteen-fifties. My childhood memories were wonderful. Our family of six consisted of my father, mother, two brothers, my sister, and me.

My dad worked in a quality control lab at a local factory Monday thru Friday. On the weekends Dad took on a second job as a security officer stationed in a guard shack checking in and out semi-truck deliveries. Dad worked hard for many long hours just to put food on our table and simply to make ends meet.

Mom was a stay-at-home mom, so we just got by. It wasn't until many years later that I really understood what we had. Our house was filled with love and was a real functioning family, a far cry from some of today's families. At times it was difficult when we went without because there was no money for extras. Our family had many unique personalities and was far from perfect, but we functioned well together.

One of my first recollections as a young boy is receiving a red bicycle, the kind with training wheels. The bike was a beautiful high gloss red and had a banana seat and black grips. You could hear the sound of my bike coming down the road. All the kids in my neighborhood used clothespins to hold the playing cards on the front forks that would brush against the spokes as the wheels turned. The clicking sounds of the cards brushing against the wheel spokes started slowly at first and gained rhythm with speed.

The wheels were solid black rubber and had no give when you the hit the bumps in the road. The ride jolted my spine with every move, but still, I was a king or an outlaw rider or maybe the police riding the neighborhood and chasing the bad guys. I was always trying to keep up with my older brothers, but they had no problem getting away from me. Being years older they had advanced to larger bike models and had gained the necessary riding skills to leave me in the dust. Still, I was part of the group at age four but always riding in the rear.

There's nothing like riding behind the group to teach you to ride faster. By the time I would catch up to them, off they would go to a new destination. Then came the day I remember my dad taking the training wheels off. Man, it was just like riding for the first time. The bike wobbled and turned back and forth and side to side. Like most things in life once you get it, you get it, and you look back in amazement wondering, *Why did this take so long?* With this freedom came a newfound self-confidence.

> Romans 12:10, GWT — "Be devoted to each other like a loving family..."

I was blessed to grow up in a time when life seemed simple. Even though Dad was gone working a lot, our family ate dinner together around our dining table because Dad loved his family (but I can't ever remember him telling me so). Dad was big and strong; he was a man's man. One of the ways Dad showed his love for us kids was to take his boys trout fishing in northern Michigan. Sometimes we fished just for the day; other times we went for a weekend camping trip. Some of the best memories of my dad were at a place we called the railroad bridge. There we would sit side by side fishing, with our lines in the water and no words spoken. It was good just being together.

Dad proudly sat on the sidelines at hundreds of my Little League games. He wasn't overly vocal, but he was watching and always making eye contact. I think as soon as I spotted him unfolding his lawn chair, a sense of security, certainty, and confidence came over me. Dad had arrived; all is right in my world, so now let's play ball.

Mom was a master at stretching a dollar by searching store ads, cutting coupons, and on Thursday evenings shopping for bargains at three or four grocery stores. Dad worked two jobs so mom could stay home and tend to our family. It's amazing to think how hard they worked for us and all the sacrifices that were made on our behalf. When families do what they do to get by, then life becomes an adventure. Those who see it that way get the little things in life that most miss.

> Matthew 8:26, ESV — "And he said to them, 'Why are you afraid, O you of little faith?'..."

Much of my free time in early childhood was spent delivering newspapers. My oldest brother Steve had the route. Steve ran his paper route like he was the head of a major corporation, or maybe like a union boss. My brother Phil and I were his workers, and work we did! Thinking back, we grew up tough. In rain or snow or whatever the weather was, seven days a week we delivered the press. The route consisted of three parts: Byron Center Avenue, Arden, and a small street that had a boy's home: the home where the troubled kids were sent to live temporarily and receive counseling to get their lives on track.

The home seemed like a large orphanage for hardened boys that acted differently than the rest of the kids in my neighborhood. These boys would watch, or rather, stare at us with mean, angry looks on their faces. This "orphanage" had five or six homes scattered throughout a wooded area and most homes received the newspaper. This section was always the most difficult area to deliver the papers to because of the large wooded spaces in between the houses.

A ton of anxiety would build within me as I approached the large white house with several mean dogs running around wild. I always needed to preplan several well-rehearsed exit strategies before entering the area. My anxiety of delivering the papers to this home would begin hours before. As the youngest brother, I was literally "thrown to the dogs" as the dogs would spot me and run after me while biting at my ankles.

Life is a process, a series of climbing and sometimes plateauing. Early on we must be guided by our self-confidence, perception, curiosity, and the desire for more. We will either grow and persevere, overcoming the difficulties of our past, or we withdraw from our future potential. Much about childhood is the confidence instilled by the parents and the self-confidence developed by the child. Through new found confidence our talents develop, our interest becomes more focused.

> Romans 12:6, NIV —"We have different gifts, according to the grace given to each of us..."

Each of us are given certain talents and gifts. Some kids understand this right away. I've admired how some kids knew they were going to be a fireman, or a doctor, a business leader, and so on. I was not that kind of kid. I was unsure about my future, partly because I've always been adaptable and good at a lot of things.

Well, I was good at playing baseball, and we played a lot of it. Every day in the summer all the neighborhood kids would meet at the field, choose teams, and play for hours. That was quite different from today's standards; it seems like a rarity to see kids outside playing catch. Of all the sports played today, baseball is still the game I love the most. Most summer days we would get on our bikes, head over to the field, and not come home for hours. Back then moms were good with this.

> Titus 2:2, GWT — "…Tell them to be men of good character…"

Perhaps thousands of summer nights I fell asleep listening to the voice of the Detroit Tigers announcer Ernie Harwell and Paul Carey calling the games. I felt like I knew Ernie more than just by recognizing his voice — we were connected through his fabulous descriptions of the play by play, which was how he connected so well with his listeners. I met Ernie as an adult and saw his love for people as well as his unashamed love for the Lord.

He was a real standup guy. It was an honor to say I had met him, and he was just like I thought he would be. It's more than chance when you meet someone in life with strong character and strong morals who is an example for others to follow. God puts such people in our path along life's way: some people see it, some people get it, but others never understand it at all.

> To have grown up in a home where my parents truly loved and cared for each other set the tone and the foundation for my life.

Some school teachers, Sunday school teachers, pastors, family members, and friends have had a profound effect on my life, steering and guiding me through tough times. However, upon entering high school, I still had no clear direction on my career as everything interested me.

James 4:14, BSB — "You do not even know what will happen tomorrow! What is your life? You are a mist that appears for a little while and then vanishes."

From my formative childhood years to the night that changed my life forever, nothing could have prepared me for what lay ahead. One very hot August night my life changed, and this event has affected my life every day since. The horror and paralyzing fear of the robbery took place on a single night, but the trials and difficulty took decades to understand and overcome.

How do you face death in the eye when you're not ready to go? I was a regular sixteen-year-old, doing sixteen-year-old stuff. I wasn't exactly a bad kid but was certainly no altar boy, either. I had a girlfriend, a car, and a part-time job; it was summer, and we were having fun.

For me, there were no quick fixes, no instant processes that would cause me to be an overcomer. Instead, in my life the power of forgiveness was a journey, causing me to come out stronger and more powerful than ever before. I chose to be an overcomer, so I could be free from the haunting memories of the past. My journey is about perseverance to push ahead and claim victory.

## CHAPTER 2 DISCUSSION QUESTIONS

---

### LIFE LESSONS

The foundation in life beings with family. To have grown up in a home where my parents loved each other instilled a childhood of self-confidence within me. Parents guide their children's future through hard-work, sacrifice, and necessary discipline. I am thankful my parents modeled a loving environment for our family.

---

## Points to Ponder

Your childhood largely influences your future; do you look back at childhood as happy or as sad times?

If you could go back and change one thing, what would it be?

If you were hurt as a child, how can you find hope for a positive fulfilling life?

Describe how you worked through the process.

Regarding physical or emotional abuse or other hurts from childhood, forgiving and trusting adults is difficult. Can you trust again?

How have you worked through the process?

# CHAPTER 3

# The Robbery

Isaiah 61:8, NIV — "For I, the LORD, love justice; I hate robbery and wrongdoing..."

*Life can change on a moment's notice; through my tragedy, in the heat of the moment, I met the God of the universe, face to face, and my life was changed forever.*

There are moments in life that just take you by surprise. All the guidance and all the preparation from your parents and teachers still does not prepare you for the unexpected. For me, the unexpected almost took my life at a moment's notice.

My first car was a 1966 baby blue Plymouth Belvedere, complete with air shocks that lifted the rear end of the car and loud header pipes with cool looking Thrush muffler exhaust that ran along the bottom of the doors. The high polish chrome mag rims with slightly larger tires on the back made this car look cool. My car was actually really slow but looked like the hot rods or muscle cars that most of my friends were driving.

This Tuesday started out like any other summer day. I was dressed in blue jeans, a bright red marine corps tee shirt, and tennis shoes. My girlfriend lived a couple of streets over, and I would drive over to her house, hang out for a while, and then head off to work.

I worked at a grocery store in the dairy department loading cheese, eggs, butter, and milk into coolers. My shift in the summer would begin at noon and end when the store closed around ten pm. The store was on the lower end for grocery stores, and the owners catered to low income and food stamp customers. The owners treated everyone with respect. They understood selling goods at rock-bottom prices, often bringing customers in from out of town and the inner city.

The store had a large wooden work table near the offices with white meat wrapping paper on a roll. Each day the store manager would use different colored markers to make homemade signs announcing the daily specials, like bananas for twelve cents a pound or fresh ground hamburger for a dollar and twenty-nine cents a pound. The signs were stapled to the exterior of the building and hung in the windows for some low-budget advertising.

This was a low budget operation, to say the least: home-made wooden shelves in white washed flat white, concrete floors painted with a high gloss battleship gray color — the cracks and pits exposed — and over time the paint coatings would fill in the low spots. After walking in, the front wood entry door would slam shut with a loud bang behind you; there was nothing automatic here. The ceilings were dotted with primitive lighting: a single bulb hung down from a lone wire every few aisles. Of course, there was no air conditioning, just a few fans to blow around the hot humid air.

It was a hotter than normal work day; the temperature had risen well into the nineties. Usually, in the late afternoon, we would unload a milk, butter, and cottage cheese delivery from a local dairy. Wheeling stacks of milk crates into the cooler was a welcome relief from the oppressive heat.

As the afternoon turned to evening, all was normal in the store, or so I thought. The last few customers completed their purchases and out the door they went. My manager Walt, another coworker, Jim, and I locked the doors.

There had been some spills throughout the day that customers had tracked through and left footprints and wheel tracks on the painted gray concrete sales floor. Walt gave the orders for me to get a mop bucket and clean up these areas while he and Jim counted and recorded the cash. Walt liked to have the floors looking nice for the owners when they came in the morning.

I went to the dimly lit back room, gathered the mop bucket and a ringer, and proceeded to clean up the floors throughout the store. When the cleaning was complete, I returned to the store's back room where the mop sink was located in a back corner of the stockroom. I planned on finishing this up and meeting the other guys so we could all walk out together.

Sweating and dripping wet, I entered the small mop sink area. The first task was cleaning the mop with clean water, wringing it out, and then hanging it to dry on the nail on the wall. Then as usual, I faced into the corner, and picked up the mop bucket, leaning the bucket on the edge of the sink as I dumped the dirty water.

Taking the rubber garden hose, I swished the water around and gave one last rinse, watching the last of the grains of sandy dirt stream into the drain. As the last of the water spilled into the sink basin, I reached to turn off the water, when without notice and with no time to react, my life changed forever. Unknown to me, two robbers were hiding in the darkness of the back room.

In an instant, one of the robbers reached with his left hand over the top of my head, grabbed my hair, and pulled my head backward and upward at the same time. In perfect timing his right hand instantly swung and held a large knife to my throat.

The other robber grabbed my arms and held them behind my back, all the while pressing a second knife against my lower back. In one moment of time, I had a knife on both my throat and on my back. I was ambushed and completely at their mercy. They said, "Move, and we will kill you." Then the robber that held the knife at my throat screamed that same threat over and over in my ear, at least twenty times within a minute. This robber seemed crazed, while the other robber seemed much less violent, more level headed. Thankfully this other robber settled down the crazy one, or I am sure the crazy one would have killed me right there on the spot.

I felt the sharpness of the blade begin to pierce the front of my throat, and then felt a dripping down my neck and onto the front of my shirt. In just a few moments, the chest section on the front of my shirt was wet. I thought, *they have me and there is no time or any way to fight my way out of this.* They had me, and I knew it!

With my hair pulled back, my head was lifted high forcing me to look at the ceiling. The robber's constant voice repeated, "Don't look at us or I will cut your throat! I will kill you! I WILL KILL YOU! I WILL KILL YOU!" Somehow my eye met the corner of his eye, just inches away. How do I describe the pure evil I saw in an absolutely crazy person who in a split second could end my life? The intensity of rage in this guy's voice was beyond scary because first, I was in an impossible situation to defend myself and second, I was at the mercy of a guy who was out of control and out of his mind.

It was later found out the robbers were two brothers; one had worked at the store a year or so ago. The brothers were high on drugs at the time of the robbery, and it was obvious they were not in the right frame of mind.

At this point I was completely paralyzed with fear; my body and mind seemed frozen in time, almost unable to act or react to their commands. Fear overcame me. Although they gave me a command once, I heard their words echo in my ears such as "Move, move, move." The actions of moving seemed like super-slow motion, almost like an out-of-body experience or like I was watching the situation from a distance. Everything became distorted and out of shape. I now believe my mind went into extreme shock, followed by the almost useless functioning of my arms and legs. I have no idea how long I was in this state—maybe a second or two—before I snapped back into the reality of the situation.

They had me walk slowly backward, taking half, or maybe baby steps as we inched our way out of the confined area. This was so awkward—looking up at the ceiling, hair being pulled, knife against my throat, my hands held back behind me, knife against my spine. The brothers clearly had no idea what to do next. They needed to get to the office quickly before the day's receipts and cash were put into the time-released safe. Once the safe door closed, it could not be opened until the preset timer allowed it to open at eight the next morning.

The brothers came up with one idea after another on what to do with me and then would quickly change their minds again. I was not part of the original robbery plan; in fact dealing with me in the stockroom stopped everything in its tracks. The brothers had been devising their plan for some time; they would hide in the darkness of the back room, then ambush the night manager and get the cash. I was a sudden unforeseen problem. Dealing with me took valuable time out of their robbery plan.

Seconds turned into minutes and minutes seemed like hours as the brothers devised a plan on what would be best to do with me. They finally decided to tie me up. The more level-headed brother ran from the stockroom into the store, found some clothesline, and opened the package while the crazy brother kept the knife blade against my throat and continued with the "I will kill you!" threats.

Once the brother returned with the clothesline, the other brother tied my wrist and arms behind my back. My attention momentarily shifted to the continuing drip, drip, drip of liquid running down my throat, and onto the front of my red tee shirt that was now entirely soaking wet. After tying my hands behind my back, they tied my ankles together. Somehow at this point in the situation, I began to relax a bit, realizing that if they were going to kill me they probably would have already done it by now. Tying me up made me feel that I was either going to be a hostage or would be left in the stockroom so they could continue their robbery plan.

Now that I was completely tied up, the two brothers tried to quickly decide what to do with me next. Again this time spent on me was completely foiling the robbery plan. Only so much time and the safe would be shut until morning. The more reasonable brother said let's put him in the dairy cooler.

I was forced to hop into a dairy cooler about seventy-five feet away, still with a knife at my throat and a knife poking in my back. It was very difficult to do this, hopping through a dark stockroom and trying to not get killed in the process. It was a miracle I didn't stumble or trip during the stockroom journey because surely my throat and spine would have been cut wide open.

Everything was happening so fast but yet in super-slow motion as the brothers were in complete control, and I was forced to just comply. Everything within my being wanted to fight back and try to get free, but it wasn't going to happen. One of the things these brothers were skilled in was knowing how to tie somebody up. My wrists were tied so tightly that I was losing circulation in my hands, and any effort to move my hands was wearing the skin off my wrists.

## Deal Making

> Life can change on a moment's notice; through my tragedy, in the heat of the moment, I met the God of the universe, face to face, and my life was changed forever.

As I was led into the cooler, I told God, *I'm sorry for all the mistakes I've made and if you get me out of this I will serve you forever.* I thought I would do better if only God gave me another chance, a second chance. I was a typical sixteen-year-old, living life for the moment, taking advantage of everything that came my way.

I wasn't a bad teenager; I was just living life on my own terms. At some point during this bargaining, I had a vision that I was lying in a casket with my parents looking down at me, crying uncontrollably because these robbers had killed me. It was a horrible vision in my mind, and somehow I felt I let them down.

If my life had ended that night I would have been guilty. I was guilty of making poor decisions, living my life without God and without a relationship with Jesus, and living a life to please myself, full of sin and without forgiveness. That was a defining moment in my life. Once again I said, *God I'm sorry for my mistakes — God I'm sorry for the way I've been living — I promise I will change — I will live my life to honor you — forgive me Lord — forgive me Lord!* I prayed under my breath in the heat of the moment. I have no recollection of time. I'm guessing these thoughts and prayers went through my mind in a matter of a few seconds.

With the heat and humidity of the hot August night and my adrenaline pumping from the intense stress caused by hopping over to the cooler at knife point, now my red marine tee shirt was completely wet. For at least twenty minutes I had a knife against my throat, causing liquid to drip down my tee shirt. Occasionally I tried to look down to see how much blood I was losing. So I prayed and pleaded: *Please, God, don't let me bleed to death – God, please stop the bleeding – Protect me, God, protect me, God.*

Then an overwhelming fear of dying raced through my mind. In a microsecond thoughts quickly passed through my mind: Little League baseball games, my family, fishing trips with my brothers and my dad, family vacations and a whole bunch of things I'd done wrong in my short life. At lighting speed images flashed through my mind faster and faster, like movie highlights of segments of my life, each flashing for a microsecond and then on to the next scene. The robbers kept barking out orders at me as they made split-second decisions on the fly. With all this going on, I was in complete confusion.

This is how you feel when someone is completely controlling you – this is life and death, right here and right now. I thought, *My life is in God's hands – why am I going through this – what's the purpose?* Then my mind flashed back to survival mode and complying with their orders so I could stay alive.

As the brothers pushed me into a thirty-eight-degree dairy cooler, I saw their faces for the first time since this ordeal started. I just stared at their faces of evil. They shouted at me to look away or they would kill me. With that they slammed the door shut, locked the door, and then dragged cases of merchandise in front of the door to prevent my escape.

Behind the closed door, I could hear their footsteps become more and more distant until there was pure quiet. Quickly my thoughts shifted from myself to my co-workers. I began to fear for Walt and Jim because they were about to get ambushed and possibly experience worse things than I did. They also would be changed for life. I quickly began to pray for their safety.

Now left alone in the cooler, I began to explore my surroundings. I could hop around a little but still was unable to untie my wrists or ankles. I soon began to shiver uncontrollably from the sudden temperature change and the anxiety caused by the robbery. Then I realized I could finally look down at my shirt. The red marine tee shirt was soaking wet, yet God answered my prayer. My shirt was not wet with my blood, it was wet from the sweat dripping down my neck! What a relief it was to discover my neck had not been slashed and I was safe, for the time being.

## Totally Soaked, Very Cold, and Alone with God

> Deuteronomy 31:8, NIV — "...he will never leave you nor forsake you..."

My thoughts were scattered. I was safe for now, but I worried about the safety of my co-workers. My mind imagined the worst scenarios. I continued making the deal with God, in my immature way. Then my thoughts wandered. I was sure no matter what the future held, I would begin my new spiritual journey, and I would be a better person. I shivered and wondered again about the other guys. Slowly the time passed, from ten minutes, to fifteen, to thirty, to forty. The more time passed, the more worry came over me along with guilt for not being able to warn the others of the robbers and the danger. I also felt guilty for not helping them, but truly there was nothing I could do except pray for their safety and that things would be okay.

Walt and Jim were busy counting the cash, checks, and food stamps, while the robbers used their valuable time getting me out of the way. The typical time to count the cash was about twenty minutes. Next Walt and Jim sorted the money for the day and completed the necessary documentation for the next day's deposit. Walt opened the safe, Jim handed Walt the cash, and Walt placed the money in the safe. Just as the safe door closed, the brothers rounded the corner and rushed into the cash office.

Amazingly the robbers were too late to steal the safe's contents! Catching Walt and Jim by surprise, the brothers demanded the safe be opened. Walt said the safe was on a time release and once closed it would not open until 8:00 AM the next morning. Hastily the robbers tied up Walt and Jim in the cash office after stealing the cash Walt and Jim had in their wallets and then they ran from the store.

Walt and Jim were worried about me, thinking I had been killed in the back room. As soon as the robbers left, Walt and Jim got busy trying to escape. They were placed back to back, enabling them to use each other's hands to loosen and eventually to untie each other. First Jim was able to free Walt, and Walt then called the police.

My thoughts were beginning to settle down a little now. I was still nervous, freezing cold, unable to untie myself, alone, and waiting to be freed. For a while, I tried to make sense of the situation, and then I wondered about the other guys. Walt was a grandfatherly figure to us younger guys, and I believe he cared deeply for us. He was a fun older guy and enjoyed a good laugh, not all business-like. He had spent his entire working career in the grocery business. After about twenty-five minutes, the wetness of my shirt compounded by the refrigeration unit blowing cold air down on me made me shiver uncontrollably.

With the sound of the refrigeration unit fans blowing inside the cooler it was difficult to distinguish the sounds on the inside from the sounds on the outside of the cooler. I recall hearing the sounds of footsteps running toward the cooler door. My heart skipped a few beats, and I thought the robbers were coming back for me, maybe to take me hostage or to kill me. But the approaching footsteps continued past the cooler and grew fainter until they were gone. Once again all was quiet. This added to the confusion of the night.

Suddenly I heard yelling, commotion, and screaming! My first thought was the robbers were coming back to cut me up. Wow, how quickly my new-found faith faded as fear instantly rushed in. There were sounds of many footsteps running by the outside of the cooler. Then all of a sudden the police kicked the cooler door in, with guns drawn and pointed at my face! At that moment the police did not know if I was one of the robbers. They yelled, "Hands up, hands up!"

I stood looking into the end of the two policeman's revolvers with the hammers cocked maybe thirty inches from my face. Once again extreme fear rushed over me that now by accident I could be killed. I told them my arms were tied behind my back. One officer kept the gun on me while the other officer checked my hands.

The impact of the police startling me and holding me at gun point was as scary as the robbery itself until I recognized I really was being rescued. The look in Walt's eyes when he saw I was safe was unforgettable. At last, we were all united, hugging, and high-fiving, excitedly telling our part of the story until we filled in all the details of the previous forty-eight minutes.

As the story of the night's events unfolded, the running footsteps past the cooler were the robbers leaving the store the same way they had come in, through the stockroom back door. The past forty-eight minutes of my life had changed me forever, and I would soon begin the long road to recovery.

I called my parents, who were already in bed for the night, telling them I would be late coming home. They didn't seem overly concerned, but they were happy no one was hurt. The three of us went to the police station and spent hours being interviewed by several detectives. We told and retold the events of the night. Then through some excellent police work, the word came into the interview room that the robbers had been caught, arrested, and were in custody in the police station! The night ended with the suspect lineup and the three of us identifying the robbers. I drove home about 2:30 AM, a different person, innocence removed at the hands of two robbers.

God protected me as I asked Him to. I had several cut lines on my throat that only looked like scratches on my skin. The cuts were so insignificant, but during the robbery felt much worse because of the sweat that dripped into the wounds, making my skin burn from the irritation. They quickly healed and disappeared in a day or two. Both of my wrists had rope burns from my constant effort of trying to free myself, but once again God caused the skin to heal in just a few days.

## CHAPTER 3 DISCUSSION QUESTIONS

---

### LIFE LESSONS

The robbery shook me to the very core of my being. My mind cannot make sense of the forty-eight minute ordeal. The robbery took me through the greatest of fears believing I was going to be killed, held against my will and the shame of not being able to defend myself. Through the trauma I cried out to my God, and He met me right where I was at. I was safe no matter the circumstances, I gave my heart to Him, and that moment changed the course of my life forever.

---

## Points to Ponder

Has your life ever changed on a moment's notice? Many times we fight the feelings of taking revenge or becoming angry. How have you dealt with these feelings? Did you choose to begin moving toward forgiveness?

The aftermath of tragedy will cause you to either grow or regress. How has your life changed? Explain the positives and negatives of how your life has changed from a traumatic event.

Did your experience bring you into deeper faith? If so explain how God worked in your life through these events.

## CHAPTER 4

# Finding Forgiveness Thirty-Eight Years Later

Mark 11:25, NIV—"And when you stand praying, if you hold anything against anyone, forgive them, so that your Father in heaven may forgive you your sins."

*The act of forgiveness is the submission of your will, your first step toward freedom.*

This morning I was up early; the alarm went off at 4:15 AM! After a quick shower and a cup of coffee, my wife and I were ready to leave the house. A check of the weather showed it was –8 degrees Fahrenheit with a light dusting of snow that had arrived overnight, requiring the plane be de-iced before takeoff. Leaving our frigid Michigan home this early will be worth the effort because in a few hours we will be walking out of a plane and into 75 degree Florida sunshine. It will be pure heaven.

Vacations are a wonderful part of life. Getting away from everyday routines and work helps me to wind down.

Throughout most of my life it has been difficult for my mind to relax. The post-traumatic stress from the robbery adds to the way I process information. Traumatic moments are significant in the years they happen and decades later. The hurts and abuse in my life and/or in other victims lives hide deep in memories that easily go back to childhood or teen years.

This was going to be a typical trip for us. My wife Robin normally shops for our Southwest Florida Gulf Coast rental condo, air fare, and rental car six to nine months in advance. Since we have been traveling to the same general area for years, we already have in mind some favorite restaurants, clothing stores, and activities for the week. There was so much to look forward to, so much to do, including walking along the gulf in the surf in the warm Florida sunshine. We have carefully trained and developed our company staff to work and understand our business, so our years of investing into them has brought us to this point.

As I boarded the plane, I gladly left the stress of work behind and a sense of relief came over me. What an amazing feeling! As the plane gained altitude, I reached for my computer to write about life adventures. I thought about my early childhood. How blessed I was to grow up in a loving family with the feeling of well-being. Knowing I was loved and cared for was good for my soul. So I began to write stories of my childhood experiences: summer picnics with grandparents, camping trips with my dad and brothers fishing for trout in northern Michigan.

I was blessed to grow up with fond memories from my childhood. Delivering newspapers taught us boys a valuable work ethic. Something as simple as the newspaper brings real enjoyment to the readers, while some customers waited for their deliveries, greeting us most days.

Somewhere life begins to change from being a paperboy to getting a first real job. Like a lot of kids, I started at McDonald's and then went on to a grocery store. There I bagged customers' orders, wheeled and loaded them into car trunks, and said goodbye to the customer until the following week.

Unwittingly, my writing begins to take on a serious note as I start to journey into my time at the grocery store. I wrote many details about the robbery, the most painful and difficult time of my childhood. Creative writing has always been a form of therapy for me as I record the details and settle out the difficult memories from that night.

But try as I might–after thirty-eight years–I still didn't have peace in my heart about that hot August night. I always had an unsettling in my spirit about the whole event. I grew up in a blue-collar middle-class family. Our family never sought counseling for deep-seated issues. Issues were rarely talked about or brought up. In a sense, we coped by suppressing our feelings. Over time these bruised feelings created frustrations that were difficult to deal with.

As I became an adult, there were clues I had some unfinished business. Writing gave me a sense of release from any internal frustration that had built up over the years.

As I wrote I remembered the deal I made with God: that if He safely got me out of the robbery situation, I would serve Him forever. I have kept my end of the bargain every day since. I even formally accepted Christ into my heart at eighteen years old by walking to the altar and praying a sinner's prayer in a small church in Grand Rapids, MI.

My new walk wasn't perfect. In the years to come, I made plenty of mistakes, as I think most people do. However, I have grown stronger in my faith, and I believe God is pleased and is using me in ministry opportunities.

Over the years the robbery events would give me nightmares, or certain situations would trigger the memories and make me seriously uncomfortable. Still, at fifty-eight years old, I awake in the night once or twice a month with the sensation of something pressing on my throat and the feeling I am being choked.

> 2 Corinthians 5:7, NIV — "For we live by faith, not by sight."

Wanting relief, time and again I would go to the altar and ask God to heal me of these unpleasant memories. The memories would cease for a while and then rush back into my mind. I would ask God, *Why, why can't I be healed of this event and get it out of my mind for good?*

Pausing from my writing for a few moments, again I asked God, Why can't I get this out of my mind? Then I heard God speak to me in a very clear voice, *Forgive those who have wronged you, just as I have forgiven you.* I sat still and quiet, waiting and collecting my thoughts. *Forgive these guys who caused me so much trauma and unrest for most of my life? This has caused me so much pain that I have never even told my two adult sons about this. I have only mentioned that something serious happened to me when I was sixteen.*

I guess this must be how combat war veterans feel. Trauma is the same whether it occurs in war or occurs from being victimized by criminals; it was just easier to keep it inside. Maybe it was a man's way of dealing with things because a man's pride is a pretty big deal. It was certainly the way I was brought up.

Showing signs of weakness wouldn't be cool. To open one-self up to others is just too difficult, and more importantly, unless you had been there you just wouldn't understand. Also growing up in our family we didn't seek help. We just dealt with it ourselves and stuffed it down deep inside. Truth be told, I never thought about it on purpose; it was always somewhere tattooed into the recesses of my brain and came out at the most inopportune times.

How do you just let go of thirty-eight years of memories? To better understand this, it's like life before and life after an event. Most of us can remember where we were when important specific events occurred like when my father died and another time losing a close friend. The mind can immediately recall what was happening the moment or moments leading up to these events. The brain can remember a specific song that was playing at that moment or the exact time, like my robbery took place at 10:12 PM.

> The act of forgiveness is the submission of your will, your first step toward freedom.

Forgiveness is a big decision that brings release to internal turmoil. The act to forgive or not forgive is personal to the individual who has been victim-ized by another or by the circumstances of life. Not forgiving allows the injurer to hold power over the injured, producing a self-imposed prison of anger, resentment, revenge, regret, and bitterness. This sour seed grows and develops over time within the victim's heart and spills out into their attitudes toward life and other people.

For me the decision to forgive was as easy or as hard as I wanted to make it. Nobody told me I had to do it. But I knew I heard God's voice, and He did tell me I needed to forgive if I wanted to be free from the memories. So I did it—right then and there—in a plane at thirty thousand feet altitude, flying toward Florida on a cold January day. I forgave the men who hurt me, deep on the inside of my being. The years from a sixteen-year-old to the man I have now become, I needed to give this up to God, and allow Him to begin His healing inside of me.

> Ephesians 1:2, NIV—"Grace and peace to you from God our Father and the Lord Jesus Christ."

I bowed my head and said, *God, I don't know who those brothers are, if they are alive or dead, if they are in prison or where ever they are. I forgive them for what they have done to me. I forgive them taking away teenage innocence when my life should have been filled with fun, learning, and growing into adult manhood. I forgive them for the fears that are deep inside of me, all birthed out of the dimly lit back-room trauma.*

Suddenly the plane slowly lifted maybe five hundred to a thousand feet. I instinctively felt that what happened in the natural mirrored what just took place in the spiritual. The very heavy weight and burden of shame that I had carried for decades were instantly taken off my shoulders and lifted out of my body. The memories and the horror of that hot August night were removed in an instant. Because I chose to forgive the brothers who wronged me, I was liberated and set free — like walking out of prison a free man.

## CHAPTER 4 DISCUSSION QUESTIONS

LIFE LESSONS

In life there are moments like getting married or having children that rank up there at the very top. Finding forgiveness is truly the most important event of my life. Forgiveness between God the Father and me is an amazing relationship that words cannot describe. Forgiving others who hurt me allowed my life to change course, from being angry and bitter to giving them to God and releasing the weight I carried on my shoulders. Living my life in the freedom that forgiveness provides.

## Points to Ponder

It's easier to be mad at people than forgive them; what does that mean to you?

Forgiving someone takes courage; have you ever forgiven someone who has hurt you?

Has someone taken away your innocence, which can mean many different things; what does it mean to you?

Have you been able to forgive them, or have you been able to forgive yourself?

# CHAPTER 5

# The Power of Forgiveness
# Modern Times

2 Corinthians 5:17, ESV — "Therefore, if anyone is in Christ, he is a new creation. The old has passed away; behold, the new has come."

*Your identity is not your position in life, job titles, net worth, or degrees. Your identity is in Jesus Christ — nothing more, nothing less.*

How do you understand forgiveness? Does the power of forgiveness begin at the cross?

On the cross of Jesus Christ, over two thousand years ago, He gave His life for you and me. Understanding forgiveness starts here.

I could never have forgiven the brothers who victimized me without first understanding what Jesus did for me. Year after year I prayed the horrifying memories to be erased from my memory, but the truth is, it's part of my life story. It is the reason for me writing this book, to share my story and the story of my healing.

In the weeks after the robbery, I had almost celebrity status to my friends and coworkers. People would ask me to tell and retell the story of that night. I would give my side of the story, and Jim would add in his side of what had happened, playing off each other's version. I had never known anyone who had been through something like this, so it was fun to tell the story as we entertained the others.

The truth of the matter was, deep down inside of me, I was screaming for help. In the mid nineteen seventies my parents never would have considered taking me to counselor and talking out the night's events. You swallowed hard and toughed it out; it was the old school way of doing things. Today I understand that I suppressed some bad feelings and succumbed to some fears, but the recurring nightmares continued for decades.

Decades passed without really knowing or understanding how to deal with these feelings. The old memories become a way of life. My mind reverted back to some types of fear in dark confined spaces that just plain and simple make me very uncomfortable. God was my healer of this madness, and being strong and committed to a more normal future drove my will to overcome the past events of the robbery night. It continues to drive my will today.

The crimes against another person come from the physical or from the emotional hurt and abuse or both. I have heard story after story where a young child was sexually abused by an older sibling for years and no one steps in to stop it only to be followed up by the father beating the mother in front of the children or then only to begin beating the children themselves.

Abuse always runs downhill; hurting people hurt other people, and the abusers look for the weakest person who won't defend themselves. Abusers are often fueled by some form of substance abuse that gives power and courage to the abuser.

How do you go about forgiving someone who has hurt you or forgiving yourself for a decision you made years ago? Let's look at a few examples that can set you free. Imagine you were an adopted child; somewhere in childhood your mother decided, *I don't want you anymore* and dropped you off at an orphanage or into the foster care system. The guilt you might feel can be overwhelming. And the question in your mind would be why, why didn't my mom love me, why did she give me up? The feeling of being abandoned might be overwhelming, or the feeling I am not a natural-born child in this family; I don't fit in like the other kids. The aspect of forgiveness is forgiving the mother who gave you up. The decision to forgive the mother would be almost impossible without God's help; most people could never get to the point to forgive.

The other side of the coin is the mother, who at a difficult time in her life became pregnant. The mother most likely has overwhelming feelings of insurmountable guilt from either giving up a child for adoption or perhaps ending her pregnancy. Under most circumstances the mothers don't see past their current circumstances; life is just simply far too overwhelming to look into the next moment, hour, or even a day ahead.

> Your identity is not your position in life, job titles, net worth, or degrees. Your identity is in Jesus Christ — nothing more, nothing less.

Several times I have heard my pastor say to our congregation that when faced with tough times, God can turn around any situation in the next twenty-four hours. Your faith and prayers can allow something to happen if we give it to God and let Him do it. Sometimes we quite simply give up far too early on our situation or maybe our dreams when faith tells us breakthrough is just around the corner.

The mother in this example can simply ask God for forgiveness but might also begin to look inward at herself first. The answer to *"Why did I do this?"* might simply be *"I was overwhelmed and did not know where to turn. I was all alone, afraid and thru my eyes saw no way out."*

Maybe in an unplanned pregnancy, the man is just not there, or if he is, he may be unwilling to accept responsibility for his child. In a moment of crisis, what will she do? It might depend on her ability to cope, her family, friends, or support system. Regardless of the why, forgiveness might start with forgiving herself, reconciling the fact that everyone makes mistakes. In the above example, a single woman with an unplanned pregnancy is serious business, but as we do in most instances in life, we take ourselves far too serious.

Time and time again, I have heard the story of the young boy that was promised by his father: *I will pick you up on Friday after school. We will go fishing together on Saturday morning.* Billy sits on the front porch with his weekend bag, fishing pole, and tackle box only to wait and wait for the dad that never comes. The minutes turn to hours, daylight turns to darkness, and dad doesn't come for his son. The mother comforts the young boy the best she can, but the disappointment and the hurts run deep, deep into his soul.

As Billy grows up he has learned he cannot trust his dad, and Billy grows angry on the inside and develops a hardness of his heart. How can Billy forgive his father for letdown after letdown in his young life? In his heart, Billy continues to hold out hope that his dad's promises will come true. Realistically can young Billy work on forgiving his dad for the continued letdowns? More times than not Billy's hurt turn into anger from the constant disappointments.

Like back in chapter one where I wrote about young boys that are angry, they will find a way to release it in vandalism or perhaps gang affiliation where they have a sense of belonging. Nothing in life is more important than spending time — lots of time — with your children.

Sexual abuse is one of the most difficult of circumstances to overcome. There are stories after stories of young girls' lives touched by a relative. The abuse goes on for years, yet no one steps in to stop the abuse. Sometimes a father or an uncle somehow were given a free pass to touch her for their own pleasure, while the mother stands by and says nothing; the mother does not defend the daughter for fear of making a family scene.

Bad decisions allow this behavior to be swept under the rug to hopefully be forgotten, but the nightmare continues to live out in the minds of innocent children years and decades into the future, sometimes through their own sexual behaviors or abuse of their own children. When a young girl's innocence is lost, it is lost forever, at the hands of the people that were in her life to protect her from harm and danger, from the people in this world she trusted. How do these girls find it in their hearts to forgive the misdeeds of trusted adults? There are tens of thousands of circumstances and situations where people are hurt let down at the hands of others.

If we can see past our set of circumstances and know God is there, He will bring hope and comfort to the hurting. The God of the universe cares for you; He loves you more than we can understand. Allow Him in to begin healing the wounds.

If we can let go of self or ourselves, we can understand the love that God has for us is enough, more than enough. It is a cup overflowing with His love and grace and mercy. The world speaks the opposite message to us: have it your way, live for the moment, buy that the new car; the latest beauty trend will bring happiness. But usually, material items are a short-term fix.

The beauty of God is in forgiveness. We serve a big God who is willing to forgive; all we have to do is just call on His name. Some people might think submitting to God is a sign of individual weakness, when in fact the opposite is true. God is an all-loving, all-caring God who will meet your every need. He knows what you have gone through; just call on His name.

When I was tied up, with knives at my throat and my back, my mind recalled lots of mistakes I had made as a teenager. I called out to God, "Get me out of this, and I will serve you forever." I called out, and He delivered me out of the hands of the enemy. My freedom came when I chose to forgive those who had wronged me. My forgiveness came when I asked Jesus into my heart. Each day I start with *Lord Jesus thank you for this day.* Each day is special, a gift from God, not like yesterday, and not like tomorrow. Live today in freedom, freedom from the past. Today is unique; there will never be another day like it.

## CHAPTER 5 DISCUSSION QUESTIONS

### LIFE LESSONS

The hurts of life come from a thousand different angles. The power of forgiveness modern times speaks to life as it is lived today. Either in physical or emotional hurts and abuse where the pain touches deep into the soul God is there to hold, comfort, and love the hurting people in this world.

## Points to Ponder

In life trust sometimes gets broken. What process do you use to trust people again, or can you trust someone again?

If you let go of yourself and let God, what does that mean to you?

When you understand that Jesus forgave you of your sins, what does that mean to you regarding others that have hurt you? Can you simply forgive and move on, or is it more complicated than that?

# CHAPTER 6

# Damaged Goods...No More

Ephesians 2:4, ESV — "But God, being rich in mercy, because of the great love with which he loved us..."

*I am not defined by my past mistakes, hurts or abuse, but rather by my future in Jesus Christ.*

It's hard to describe the change you feel in yourself after being violated at the hands of others. Somehow it hardens you, or things are just not as fun as they were before innocence was lost. The fact is when somebody takes something away from you, once it's gone, it's gone forever. You're a changed person from the one God created you to be. I have recovered as most people who have been victimized do, but there is a change that is almost impossible to describe to others. It's almost impossible to try to explain.

Damaged goods no more — that's what I proclaim for my life today. I am changed from the violence of the robbery and from the police officer's gun pointed at my face as I looked down into the barrel of his revolver. How do you plead for help and people still do not listen? The police officers refused to believe me when I could not show them my hands? They yelled; I pleaded; they yelled; I pleaded again.

It gets very confusing really fast when people order you to do something you simply cannot do. I want to forgive them, but I cannot do that... they, them, dad, uncle, brothers, robbers, unfaithful spouse or drunk driver or you name it—whatever kind of abuse you may have faced in your life. I will forgive when I am ready to. Why, why wait for someday to forgive? With the proper counseling, most issues can be worked out to find some form of positive resolution.

Maybe it's a lack of trust in humanity. My story is a story that happens thousands of times every year to thousands of people in armed robberies. My story is unique to me because it happened to me. Dreams are smashed into a thousand pieces, never to be put back together again.

> Romans 8:38, NLT—"And I am convinced that nothing can ever separate us from God's love..."

The hurt, abuse, and violence that happen each and every day are felt by the multitudes throughout the world, yet I know that I am loved by God.

What a biblical statement of enormous proportions that when trusted parents and others have let you down, I can say I am loved by God and He does love me; the Bible tells me so. Several times a year I wake from the nightmares of a knife blade held against my throat, gasping and coughing from the feeling of someone trying to kill me and holding me against my will. I can say with confidence that I am loved by God. God's peace comes over me, and the calm returns.

> Jeremiah 17:7, ESV — "Blessed is the man who trusts in the LORD, whose trust is the LORD."

Life is already hard, but life is even harder when the circumstances of violence, abandonment, hatred, and the many ways abuse can rear its ugly head. Life is not fair. The reality of life is that it is sometimes a cruel teacher that in some cases leaves little hope for the victims who have been discarded and left behind. Without hope, it is difficult to go on with life, but our hope is in Jesus Christ.

> Hebrews 13:5, NET —"I will never leave you and I will never abandon you."

In the reality of abandonment, there is hope of reconnecting, the hope in the power of forgiveness that relationships can be restored once more. The questions in someone's mind when they have been abandoned call out to unbelievable loneliness to the wife whose husband walked out on her and the children as she cries uncontrollably to try to reclaim some form of normalcy to her shattered family. Or to the children who were removed from their homes by social services in the middle of the night due to neglect or abuse.

There are literally thousands of circumstances where innocent people have been hurt, damaged, touched, or have been cheated on by the hands of others. Each story and each circumstance is unique to each individual; the hurts are real, and the hurts run deep.

The difference is how do we go on, or do we go on, or do we become locked down by the experience that hurt us. Or do we fight to regain normalcy. For some, it is as easy as, "OK it happened, and I'm moving on"; for others, it's a moment by moment battle reliving the hurts and humiliation of an abusive childhood father, uncle, or another trusted family friend.

The makeup of the individual will determine the ease or the difficulty of overcoming the past. Both the confident and less-than-confident person may struggle in their ability to overcome the past hurts and abuse.

The bank teller who went to work today just like every other day may face bank robbers who put a gun in their faces, ushered them into a back room, tied them up, and threatened to kill them. The nightmare will live on forever in the minds of the bank employees. There must be hope to be able to return to work and have a normal life.

The mere thought of forgiveness, or forgiving the person or people that hurt you is almost impossible for the mind to accept. The hurts cut clear to the bone and deeper into the heart where trust was once the norm. Trust is now a distant memory. If we choose not to forgive, normal relationships begin to warp into non-trusting relationships. The feeling is this: *I simply cannot trust anyone because I was violated at the hands of the perpetrator.*

How can I forgive the person I hate so much for hurting me? How can I even consider the thought of forgiveness? As much as it hurts, bring it to the cross, God knows how much it hurts, He watched His own son Jesus die on the cross a horrible death. God knows our hurts; God is rejected by people every day. Forgiveness begins in your heart today. I waited thirty-eight years to begin my for-giveness journey. Thirty-eight years of anger, bitterness toward two brothers who decided to rob a local grocery store one summer night.

There is no logical thinking that will bring you into for-giveness. None. The world's systems and our culture don't work that way. Revenge, personal attacks, and uncontrollable angry outbursts are the world's way of answering back to the victimizers. Over time a bitter root continues to grow on the inside of you, bitterness takes over, and resentment and anger follow close behind.

The mind says if this didn't happen to me I would be like so and so. I would have finished school or earned that college degree and became a doctor, or some other highly paid professional. I would live in that house, and be married to that person, and the story goes on and on.

> I am not defined by my past mistakes, hurts or abuse, but rather by my future in Jesus Christ.

Some people are so wounded that they withdraw into themselves; their world shrinks in around them so that all they see are their problems, and they are never able to move forward or progress out of the damage that's been done to them. The hurts are real, and they hurt more than most people can understand. Some find comfort in drugs and alcohol to medicate the mind to forget the problems. This self-destructive comfort becomes the safe place in the mind to forget the pain of the past, today, tomorrow, and the next and the next. Medicating leads to addictions of many kinds.

Think back to a man who walked this earth long ago. He was loved by everyone for most of His life, but in the end faced the utmost of rejection of all mankind. A man so hated the crowds spit on Him, whipped Him, and called Him unthinkable names.

> Revelation 21:4, KJB – "And God shall wipe away all tears from their eyes; and there shall be no more death, neither sorrow, nor crying, neither shall there be any more pain: for the former things are passed away."

That man knows the pain and disappointments we all face; He knew rejection, He knew disloyalty by His friends, and He knew being let down by others. He knew hatred, and in the end, He knew death, a humiliating death being hung on a cross.

By now you know the man I'm writing about is named Jesus. The King of Kings and the Lord of Lords, the man who takes our hurts and takes on our shame. He brings comfort to the widow, and peace to the hurting people of this world. Jesus is the one I cried out to in my time of crisis, the one who kept me safe when my life could have easily ended at the hands of the robbers that summer night. Jesus is not just a name but my Lord and Savior. Jesus is my faithful friend who has never left me or forsaken me in my times of trouble.

Jesus is the same yesterday today and forever; forgiveness begins in your heart today. The willingness to forgive the people that have hurt you is a big step; the willingness to forgive yourself for past mistakes is even bigger. Forgiveness begins with you today. Bring it to the cross and make it right because God loves you in spite of the mistakes you have made.

> Colossians 1:27, NIV — "...Christ in you, the hope of glory."

Forgiveness, as I have written before, will birth freedom inside you. Forgiveness is a process, as you will read about from my friends Pastor Moses and Diane in a later chapter. Find the way forgiveness works for you, forgive your abusers today, and again tomorrow and the next day and the next and so on to gain victory over the damage and hurts that others have caused in your life. Today is the day that I proclaim I am damaged goods no more. I believe it. I will live it and walk it out today. Today is my day of freedom. I am changed and removed from my past hurts and anxiety that others have caused me. Today I declare I am damaged goods no more.

## CHAPTER 6 DISCUSSION QUESTIONS

---

### LIFE LESSONS

Forgiving others is the first step toward moving forward. When I chose to forgive my robbers I set in motion the process to move forward. Wounded people refer back to the time or circumstances where they were wounded and cannot ever move forward. Forgiveness opens the door to moving on.

---

## Points to Ponder

Have you declared I am damaged goods no more? Explain the moment that you drew a line in the sand and said my past will no longer define who I am, or my past will not control me.

Your story is unique to you. What steps have you taken to successfully move on?

> Ephesians 4:24, NIV – "…and put on the new self, created to be like God in true righteousness and holiness."

I am a new creation in Jesus Christ; does this change your thinking or your approach to forgiving others?

In what ways do you now see things differently?

# CHAPTER 7

# Fear of Abandonment

Matthew 19:14, NAS — "But Jesus said, "Let the children alone, and do not hinder them from coming to Me; for the kingdom of heaven belongs to such as these."

*You are adopted into God's family...*
*You are His...*
*He is yours...*
*You are loved...*
*He calls you His own...*

I know of a young couple who chose to open their home to the foster-care system. After becoming certified foster care providers their home quickly became flooded with foster care children. Sometimes in the middle of the night a call would come in, asking if they could take in another child. One particular time late on a Saturday afternoon the call came in for four children, all siblings. The children were removed from the parents' home by the local authorities.

The couple responded with a resounding, "Yes, bring the children." What an enormous undertaking for a couple that has no children of their own to instantly become a family of six. Soon the children arrived, three boys and one girl, with a few of their possessions. The children's faces were full of fear as they were received into their new home. The children came in dirty clothing and appeared to have not had a bath in weeks. The little girl's hair was a dark brown, but after washing her hair three or four times, she had beautiful blond hair.

It was off to the store to quickly purchase new proper fitting clothing and to put them to bed for the night. How does a child cope with being removed from the parents' unfit home into a new home environment in just a few hours? There's no doubt these children, along with thousands of other children, move through the foster care system facing overwhelming fear of abandonment as well as fear of the unknown.

The couple, as well as other close family members, stepped forth with love, care, and discipline for these children. This young couple is driven by their faith to love others in the name of Christ.

The road has been long and a difficult for everyone involved, from the countless times holding the children as they cried in the middle of the night when nothing could ease the pain from their constant nightmares to fears and insecurities of the past.

> Ephesians 5:2, NIV – "...and walk in the way of love, just as Christ loved us and gave himself up for us..."

How does one couple continue to give love and support to these innocent children? Simply because they are called to do this, they believe God has placed them into this position to care for, and to nurture the broken hearted and hurting lives of innocent children. It takes special people to step in during these most troubled and difficult times, to love unconditionally when lives are being torn apart.

The years of hard work are paying off, and the children are growing by leaps and bounds. In school, the children are testing above grade level with their school mates. And God's purpose is fulfilled in the couple who opened their home late one Saturday afternoon, from a prayer to be used to help others to a life well lived and complete according to His purpose.

I can happily say these children are flourishing in this home and are now officially adopted by this young couple. The children are receiving ongoing counseling and will continue to receive the necessary help needed in the years to come.

The birth parents' home was in such deplorable condition due to filth, pet waste, and drug paraphernalia that the authorities ordered the home to be bulldozed over as soon as the children were removed.

These particular children were abused and neglected. What brings a parent to pursue their own needs to abuse drugs to the point that kids ages one to seven have to fend for themselves? A seven-year-old girl was now responsible for feeding and changing a baby as if she was the mother. This is a cultural problem that knows no economic or social boundaries. It's not an inner-city problem or a rural problem; it's a widespread problem everywhere.

> Romans 8:15, KJB — "For ye have not received the spirit of bondage again to fear; but ye have received the Spirit of adoption, whereby we cry Abba, Father."

Adopting one child won't change the world. But for that one child, the world will change; children are the casualties caught in the crossfire of neglect. These four children are no different than the children on the streets of Detroit running in gangs without any parental guidance, tagging their piece of the turf as their own, breaking into abandoned retail stores, and experimenting with drugs as their parents have modeled.

The four children adopted by the young couple were fortunate to have had social services step in before further damage to their lives could occur. These four children are also fortunate to have been kept together as a sibling family unit and brought into a very loving home where the couple will invest thousands of hours loving them, teaching them, and guiding them into a successful future.

At some time in the future, the children may question the past circumstances of their early childhood, the memories of the time they were removed from the birth parents' home and were dropped off at the couple's home, a time full of fear and the unknown when they were scared.

The children's lives that were filled with the fears of the past are now children in a home filled with love and security. These children have a promise of a very bright future.

These four children will always love their birth parents, and at some time in the future, the questions of their childhood will emerge. Then these kids will have the opportunity to forgive their birth parents for the abuse and neglect that took place.

> You are adopted into God's family...
>
> You are His...
>
> He is yours...
>
> You are loved...
>
> He calls you His own...

When forgiveness takes place and each child (or adult) individually makes a conscious decision to leave the past behind–to forgive those that hurt and abandoned them–it is then they will understand the power of forgiveness, which will release the hurt, fears of abandonment and neglect. Turn this pain completely over to God, allowing His healing to take place.

Crimes against children are always the most disturbing of any stories we hear. To hurt children goes beyond what the human mind can understand. Children ask for really nothing, just that their basic needs are met. All children want is to be loved, and to be safe; to them really nothing else in life matters.

Naming each type of abuse done to children would be an endless task. The hope of this book is to not call them each out specifically, but rather to recognize the signs and symptoms of hurt and abuse. It is my hope that each child or child that has grown into adulthood can pursue qualified counseling to successfully overcome a troubled past.

The victims of abandonment go far beyond children's lives to the lives of married couples where the husband or the wife has cut off the emotional needs to their spouse. This results in the emotional disconnect of living together in marriage but emotionally being a million miles away from each other. At the time, a simple hobby or interest seemed like a good and healthy thing to do, but later it can become an obsession of self-fulfillment and isolation.

The video gaming industry is quickly becoming one of the leading causes of emotional abandonment. Some men will play games with their buddies from all over the world every night until two or three AM. When hobbies become addictions, the subconscious choice has already been made between investing in the marriage relationship or something else.

The hobbies of golf, fishing, watching football, hunting, and gaming are just a few. Usually, most things done in proper balance are fine, but the emotional needs of the spouse and children must always be the top priority before the recreational needs of an individual. Again, a life lived in balance allows both marriages and relationships to grow and flourish.

The abandonment of the family causes trauma, whether by sexual immorality outside of the marriage or by the husband or the wife leaving the home because they have just given up, not wanting to be responsible or simply just not caring anymore and walking away from their spouse and children. Whatever the reasons, the lives of the ones left behind are shattered and deeply damaged.

1 Corinthians 1:9, NIV — "God is faithful, who has called you into fellowship with his son, Jesus Christ our Lord."

It is never too late to turn your life around. There is hope in Jesus. He can and will rebuild lives that have been torn apart. This is where forgiveness is most powerful. A life in Christ is the beginning of this journey. A life lived in forgiveness will remove the hurt and shame caused by others to a life lived with passion, vision and an amazing future.

## CHAPTER 7 DISCUSSION QUESTIONS

> ### LIFE LESSONS
>
> The fear of abandonment can have many applications from children that were given up for adoption to children who were removed from unfit parents home. Or perhaps a wayward husband or wife who walks away from the responsibilities of their spouse and children. God loves the hurting and lonely, He can fulfill the emotional hurts and abandonment caused by others.

## Points to Ponder

Abandonment can happen in many ways from innocent children with no parents to families where a spouse has walked out. Have you ever experienced hurts from abandonment?

Did a family member or a close friend emotionally abandon you? How did you deal with the rejection and loneliness?

How have you successfully overcome these emotional hurts? List the steps that helped you on your road to recovery.

# CHAPTER 8

# Living in The Past

Philippians 3:13, NASB—"Brethren, I do not regard myself as having laid hold of it yet; but one thing I do: forgetting what lies behind and reaching forward to what lies ahead..."

*In relationships, family dynamics, hurts, and abuse you can never change the past. Seeking help, being healthy, and living intentionally are the keys to a successful life.*

*On your good days, on your less than good days, and on days when you have had some failure, God loves you just the same. He removes your guilt and shame. Accept His love, and move on from your past mistakes. He has removed them, and so should you.*

We limit ourselves by living in the past. The devil wants to keep you from fulfilling God's promises in you by keeping you focused on the past. God loves you, and He will redeem something bad in your past and use it for your good in the future.

Do not dwell on the past, live in the past, or go on reliving and grieving the events of past. That is easier said than done. When I walk into a dimly lit space, I can feel the uneasiness begin to unnerve me. I must make a conscious effort to control my emotions to stay strong in spite of my past circumstances.

One of the barriers to forgiveness is living in the past; many people cannot move beyond mistakes of their past. Maybe there is comfort for them here; perhaps it's like an old friend who is always there. People tend to think of their memories as better than what they really were. I remember the good old days when life was a much simpler time. A time when we sat on the porch with Uncle Bill and Aunt Mary, sipping ice tea and watching the fireflies come out after dark. We would talk for hours. The mind can take you back to a moment in time of pleasure, of peace, or of good times. However, the mind can take you back to the difficult times as well, times of failure, fear of a time where you were hurt or scared or maybe a time of regret.

Living in the past is exactly that, living in today's world while looking back at a past mistake or an earlier time or a time of several mistakes. Mistakes can rock your world and will paralyze you into making any logical decision with confidence. Living in past will dictate most, if not all, future decisions. The difficult part here is living within one's own-self-confidence and not living up to your own God-given potential.

Being paralyzed by fear results in making fear-based decisions. When doing a closed store inspection in Detroit, walking into the dark closed retail sales floor, I was paralyzed with fear. I believe just about anybody would have been scared out of their wits walking into that place. Still, I continued into the darkness, doing my job. More than once I wanted to turn and run to break the door down and get out of there. However, I needed to take control of the situation. I faced my fears head on and continued. That was a defining moment for me; when you persevere, the personal growth comes. I was determined to not live in the past, in the unpleasantness of the darkness. I chose to push on and push forward. I needed to do it for me and me alone.

To fully recover from the past hurts and abuse, you may need to look into how you can grow. It may be finding a trusting pastor or counselor. I do not recommend doing it my way. I was there, I pushed forth into the darkness, and it worked for me. I could have been hurt or killed inside that building that day—that was my risk I chose to take. But choosing to face my fears that day was part of my healing process. If I had turned around and never went into do that inspection that day, it would have meant that fear still had a hold on me and was controlling me to the point of not doing my job.

Not doing that inspection that day would have been the safest thing for me to do. My growth is a choice, and that growth that day was one step in the overcoming process. My past will not define me; the robbers holding me hostage will not define me; being tied up will not define me. I am living forward and not looking or living back because my future is in God's hands. I am choosing to be free and live free of those memories.

I believe in taking calculated risks where the value of the risk must have a greater reward than the consequence. Is it safe? Will it bring growth? That's the balancing act in the steps ahead for everyone choosing safety because fear of the past can lead to failure.

I will do this because it's the safest thing to do. The safety in not failing is usually the easiest path. Choosing to do nothing would hold me back from reaching my potential. Dealing with past mistakes through a certified counselor will begin the proper coping skills necessary to move forward. Again, we are human beings and all human beings make mistakes.

To start the process, we need the ability to forgive ourselves and others in our past and the past circumstances of hurt and abandonment caused by others. We need to look deep inside ourselves at the hurt we may have caused to others in our life.

The issues are complex. There are thousands of life circumstances that bring us to forgiveness. Forgiveness can work in three parts: first, to the person who had an injustice done to them, second, to the person who did the wrong to the other person and third, to the innocent bystanders who are the sum of the collateral damage that's been done by other people's actions.

Children are usually the least thought about when adults wander off into sexual immorality outside the family home. Children are highly adaptable and can and will adjust to changing circumstances quickly. But God has other plans, plans for moms and dads to love each other to live in the same home, with love, peace, and harmony as a family unit. So often the children become pawns in the custody games that are played out in the court's systems. The child's security is broken, and the model for the family and the family home is irreparably damaged.

For example, let's at look at an unfaithful spouse. When the husband chose to have an affair outside of his marriage, the wife has been hurt, the children have been hurt, and the woman who is also involved in the affair may also have a husband and children.

Once the decision has been made to have the affair, the husband has hurt his wife and children. To have any chance at reconciliation the affair must stop, the husband must confess this mistake to his wife, he must ask the wife for forgiveness, and he must forgive himself. He must also ask for forgiveness before God.

The damage caused by the above example is most difficult for couples to get through. The trust and bond of marriage made before God has been broken. Counseling and God's grace and forgiveness offer a chance at reconciliation. The complexity of human relationships brings the need for properly trained pastors and counselors where marriage vows have been broken when an affair has taken place. This is serious business and needs to be addressed with strict confidence to create a plan for healing, reconciliation, and forgiveness to take place.

Through the thousands of examples that could have been written about in this book, each situation is unique and individual to you. Your hurts are important to you; they are uniquely yours. Your life is your life; no one else on the planet has shared your exact unique experience. Yet, many people have similar experiences, and much can be learned from others.

> In relationships, family dynamics, hurts, and abuse you can never change the past. Seeking help, being healthy, and living intentionally are the keys to a successful future.
>
> On your good days, on your less than good days, and on days when you have had some failure, He loves you just the same. He removes your guilt and shame. Accept His love, and move on from your past mistakes, He has removed it, and so should you.

Forgiveness is individual; no one can do it for you. I cannot imagine where my life would be if I chose to not forgive the robbers in the grocery store. The moment I chose to forgive brought freedom from past memories, freedom from dark spaces, and freedom from looking back and living and reliving those moments. Fears have been removed. I stand as a successful husband, father, and business owner because I chose to forgive and live a life of forgiveness in Jesus Christ.

Choosing not to forgive is like taking a poison pill and hoping it hurts the other person. Forgiveness can be a difficult process for some and easier for others. For me, it was difficult to think that I would let these guys off the hook. It was much easier to hold anger and resentment in my heart against the robbers who violated me that night than to offer them forgiveness. It was a crutch for me to hold on to, the built-in excuse to hide behind in times of difficulties.

I have control over my past. My past does not define me; it's part of my life story and a small part of my future. In forgiving the brothers who violated my youth, today I pray for them. I pray that they will meet the God of forgiveness, that their lives are made clean by the forgiveness of their sins, the forgiveness that only Jesus Christ can bring into their lives. I believe this is the complete circle of forgiveness, forgiving the violators in your life, bringing them before the Lord Jesus Christ, and praying that their lives are redeemed. For me this was no small task; as I said earlier in this book, it took me about thirty-eight years to get me to this point.

Looking back, this moment it is one of the most dramatic times in my life. The robbery, the knives on my throat and back, the screaming in my face and in my ears *I'm going to kill you, mother f......*on and on twenty or thirty times in a one-to-two-minute period of time. I was defenseless, caught off guard, and my life completely in their hands. Wow, I forgive them, Lord. How powerful is this? I have freed myself from these memories by forgiving them. Jesus died to give you life and life more abundantly.

Think about the word *abundance*. Webster's says it is more than what's needed. To have more of life than what's needed would be life living and overflowing with much more than you need. Think for a minute about your life and having more of everything. Of course the Bible is speaking in a spiritual sense; all your spiritual needs are not only met but overflowing, full of the goodness of what God has to offer.

That offer comes in the form of relationship with Christ Jesus. Relationship is more than a one-person deal; it takes at least one more person to be in relation with to have the relationship. Your Christian walk begins with Jesus. This happens by desiring to be forgiven; the Bible says we each have sinned and fallen short of the glory of God.

Joshua 24:15, NIV — "...But as for me and my household, we will serve the LORD."

Let's begin the new walk with Christ. We do it by asking God the Father, Jesus the Son, and the Holy Spirit for forgiveness. We were born into this world with a sinful nature. Sin began in the Garden of Eden when Eve disobeyed God and ate from the tree of good and evil. Eve ate from the tree and felt ashamed and tried to hide from God.

In Adam and Eve's time and in our time, there is no hiding from God, who knows all things. When we die, we will be accountable for our life — the good, the bad, and the ugly.

By asking God to forgive your sins, and by accepting Jesus Christ into your life, your past is gone, you have been forgiven, and you are a new person in Christ. The angels in heaven rejoice each time a new person accepts Jesus into their hearts and is saved. When I chose to forgive the robbers as I prayed on the airplane, the plane lifted into the air gaining altitude, and it felt like thousands of pounds were lifted off my shoulders.

The question to ask yourself is what are you carrying around with you: guilt from some bad decisions? Maybe you hurt someone, or you just simply need to accept Jesus as the Lord and Savior. The need is there, and the need is real; imagine the guilt is gone the shame has been removed, and you are forgiven. The guilt of our mistakes lays blameless before the Father.

Prisons are filled with people who need forgiveness, either behind bars or in their minds.

Does guilt keep us trapped? Do we desperately desire to be free from it? Is it holding us back from finding our true identity? Do we feel we have been so bad that we cannot be forgiven? That's the lie from the pit of hell. God desires us to be free, free in Him. Accept nothing less than the truth that sets you free.

## CHAPTER 8 DISCISSION QUESTIONS

> ### LIFE LESSONS
>
> Learning to overcome hurts and mistakes helped me to move forward in my life. Living in the past is exactly that, living at a time from maybe years or decades ago. To move on meant leaving the past behind and look for new opportunities that the future holds.

### Points to Ponder

When a traumatic event happens in our lives, it is easy to live in that moment for a period of time. Describe how you have moved on from the past.

The hurts in life are real and personal to you. List the steps to successful living that helped you overcome the past.

Guilt holds people back. Explain how you gained victory over the guilt of the past.

# CHAPTER 9

# Conquering Fear

2 Timothy 1:7, NLT — "For God has not given us a spirit of fear and timidity, but of power, love, and self-discipline."

*You were created to live a vibrant life, full of opportunities and without fear.*

After the robbery, our family farm was both a place of peace and sometimes a place of fear. More specifically after it got dark, it made me uncomfortable at times. We did a lot of deer hunting and some spring turkey hunting. When we hunted, we left the safety of our truck in the early morning darkness and walked into the woods. Sometimes we would walk out in the late afternoon, sit until after sunset, and walk back to the truck after dark.

My brother, my son, and I usually hunted together; we would meet by the barn and prepare our gear. We would have a brief discussion about wind direction and each choosing our preferred tree stands and how long we might plan on sitting on our hunt.

We then will walk around the barn down a two track farm road using our flashlights, we would reach the spot where we would stop and bump knuckles whispering good luck and be safe, then each off to their assigned tree stands.

## Facing Your Fears

Most people who have survived traumatic events in their lives overtime understand the warning signs and have some sort of coping steps in place. People should try and get into the habit of avoiding any situations that cause them increased stress and difficulty. Anytime it's needed seek certified counseling.

With my flashlight pointed downward with each step, the shadows from the trees moved, brush touched against my legs, and sometimes a low-hanging branch or cobweb would touch me on the face or brush against my throat. It's in those unplanned moments that sent my heart rate off the chart until I can make sense of my surroundings. To this day I dislike anything touching my throat. I cannot even button a top shirt near my neck. I understand who I am. I simply just don't go there for any reason.

When my son, brother, and I would separate making our way to each of our tree stands, I would try to repeat Bible verses in my mind. The walk to my tree stand always heightens every sense in me. Each sound is differentiated from the normal sounds of daily life, like the sounds of water running in the creek or the wind in the trees.

The unanticipated sounds of walking up on a rabbit as it runs away in the brush instantly raises my heart beat until

I recognize and make sense of the encounter. Walking up on a group of deer-sized animals at close range busting through the brush breaking branches or flushing a group of turkeys roosting in the trees above my head are all surprise sounds that instantly take me back forty-two years to the robbery moment. It's not fear of the dark; it's fear of the unanticipated in the dark that is most difficult for me to deal with.

For other people, it might be driving near an intersection where a loved one was killed in an auto accident, or at another time a call came in the middle of the night that had bad news, or when a police officer came to the door to notify them of a close relative's death.

The memories of either physical abuse, sexual abuse, or countless other traumas lay hidden deeply imprinted in the brain. It's how we deal with maybe decades-old trauma that is meaningful today. Forgiveness in my life has taken me from not participating to living a full and complete life. Life is hard at times, but living life to the fullest is worth the risk; everyone needs to seek their own healing and comfort level.

> Philippians 4:13, ESV — "I can do all things through him who strengthens me."

With each step into the darkness, I repeat that truth over and over again. I can do all things through Christ who strengthens me. I would dwell on this Bible verse until I reached the safety of my stand location.

I would then begin to climb the twenty or so feet to reach the tree stand platform. Wearing a tree stand safety harness, I would secure myself for safety, then climb onto the stand, pull my bow up the tree with a rope, take my backpack off, hang it on a hanger, put an arrow in the bow, sit back in the darkness, and breathe. Breathing in the coolness of an early October morning, with the scent of the fall season, I feel so alive at this moment, consumed by the environment around me.

> You were created to live a vibrant life, full of opportunities and without fear.

It was then I felt safe; all fears were now gone. I am totally at peace. Strange as it sounds, to walk through the darkness raises all of the stockroom robbery insecurities within me, but once I am safe in the deer-stand all—and I mean all—fears have been removed.

It is then I have the most wonderful prayer time with the Lord, all is quiet, all is peaceful no sounds, just me and Him. It is where God speaks to me, and all distractions from my work and stresses of life are erased for a few hours. It sounds odd to think that to have such peace in my soul, I have to pass through the darkness and tormented memories from the forty-two years before.

It works for me. I have quiet and rest and peace of mind.

The family memories we have made are a wonderful place to be. I watched my son get his first whitetail buck, which is quite an accomplishment for a young teenager. The buck provided meat for our family to enjoy for the winter months ahead.

It's probably the same for others who have been victimized in their youth or adulthood, the issues of everyday life where close loved ones are lost to sickness or accidents. We serve a big loving God; through all the pain and heartache, He is waiting to wrap His loving arms around us.

It took years taking the early morning walks through the woods to find complete peace with the darkness. Dealing with fear is a lifetime proposition. I have chosen to live in the reality of everyday life. I cannot live life pretending that these things never happened to me; that would mean living in denial of my personal life history and suppressing memories for me would lead to greater anxiety down the road.

So either choice or unplanned incidents will take us back to moments of post-traumatic stress; the key to life for anyone is how we deal with it. Find your place of healing, find people to be with that can celebrate life with you, and find victory every step you take. Most of all leave the past behind and walk and live each and every day in forgiveness.

The thought of walking alone in the darkness immediately brings back the fear and uneasiness of the robbery; in fact, dark spaces overall make me nervous. Sometimes I say to myself, *Get over it; after all, it's been forty-two years.* What brings back the memories so instantly so quickly? I've forgiven the robbers, so all is well, right? So why am I still carrying this baggage?

I had the thoughts or feelings in my mind that the extreme stress that I was under at the moment of the robbery when I was jumped from behind, when my hair was pulled back, and when a knife was held against my throat and both of my arms were held behind my back by two people might be the cause. The incident happened in one or two seconds — I went from a happy-go-lucky moment in time of ending my work day to being caught up in a dreadful moment where my life could end at any second.

## The Tattooed Image in My Mind

Years later I can instantly recall the moment, that sudden gasp of air at that moment in life when everything went screaming out of control faster than you could blink your eye. In similar circumstances, I feel I'm back there. With that being said, I personally feel that I have successfully overcome the past I have forgiven those men, and live with a happy and thankful heart today.

The human mind *does not* completely forget these memories. Retrieving memories after traumatic experiences like natural calamities, concentration camps, and being victimized is well studied. Psychiatrists have also studied extensively on how to remember repressed memories. War veterans returning home from wartime service have seen and experienced things the human mind cannot conceive or make sense of.

## The Mental Imprint Left Behind

Traumatic memories are retrieved, at least at first, in the form of dissociated mental imprints of the affective and sensory elements of the traumatic experience. Victims have reported the slow emergence of a personal narrative that can be considered explicit (conscious) memory.

Like so many others who have been victimized along life's way, I choose to walk in my area of healing and forgiveness, doing well on the day-to-day living, feeling no ill effects of post-traumatic stress from earlier events in our lives. But when we walk near to the edge of those memories either by choice, like my early morning hunts or walking back to the truck after dark, it triggers an onslaught of memories that rush back into my mind faster than a tornado going through a farm town in rural Iowa.

When I created my company in the construction business, I did it because I like to see the quick results of my day's work. The visual results made me feel good to see progress being made as things were being built. I think most people in the construction trades feel this way.

Walking through a dark abandoned building doing a pre-inspection report of the structure in downtown Detroit was like walking right into pure hell.

I went through the building, which scared me almost to death, to be awarded the contract to do the work, supplying jobs to my employees, and profit for my company. A traumatic event or not, most people would have been scared out of their wits to do that particular closed-building inspection. Considering the events of my past, going in, completing the inspection was more than doing my job that day; it was a defining moment where I declared victory over my fear and anxiety of the darkness.

The other perspective is the unplanned events of life that take us to the edge of horrific memories. These are the times when something happens right before our eyes, either by accident or simply being in the wrong place

at the wrong time, again setting the triggers into super-
sonic speed.

## CHAPTER 9 DISCUSSION QUESTIONS

> ### LIFE LESSONS
>
> For the thousands of incidents that have etched fears into
> innocent victims lives. Conquering fear was important
> to moving forward from my past. To overcome fear
> allows growth, and growth new life into the hurting
> and abused.

### Points to Ponder

Do you still carry baggage from your past? How are you
dealing with this?

In the chapter "Walking into Darkness", I faced my fears
head on tackling the challenges of inspecting an abandoned building in Detroit. How have you faced your
fears, or have you moved on from it?

I find great peace on my farm, particularly sitting in a
tree stand. Where is your place of rest? Do you have a
specific peaceful place that you go to speak, seek, and
hear from God?

# CHAPTER 10

# Strength in Numbers

Matthew 7:1-2, NASB—"Do not judge so you will not be judged. For the way you judge, you will be judged; and by your standard of measure, it will be measured to you."

*Live to be healthy, go into the world and be a multiplier of forgiveness. Live to teach others, live to tell others your story of forgiveness. Declare, I am an overcomer, enrich others to live strong, and live intentionally, for a life well lived in Jesus Christ.*

Forgiveness starts here: The acknowledgement of the hurts and abuse of the past need to be recognized and sorted out. The ability to identify the root causes and deeper issues needs to be exposed in a confidential and secure setting with trusting valued people in close relationship.

Forgiveness has many parts. One part is asking the questions: Have I asked God for forgiveness? Are my sins forgiven? Did I confess with my mouth and believe in my heart that Jesus Christ is Lord? Is Jesus Christ my Lord and Savior of my life? Did I invite Jesus to live in my heart? Did I truly pray a prayer of forgiveness and mean it so that today is the day of salvation? Am I living forward and not looking back on my old life? If so, I will never be the same!

Today I start a new life. I am a new creation in Christ; old things have passed away, and all things have become new.

Can you see a difference in how you are living? With the prayer of salvation, all the old garbage in life is gone; mistakes of your past are gone, never to be remembered against you. God has forgiven you of your past. Where there was dread and sadness, today there is hope and joy! You are a new person with a new future. Having a relationship with Jesus is never being alone; whenever you are scared or nervous, He is there.

If the memories of the past come flooding back, He is there. Praise Him. Direct your focus on Him. If you call on Him, He will be a comfort to you. The forgiveness of your sins is powerful; love Him and be all you can be in Christ. This is the power of forgiveness through salvation.

I need to ask for forgiveness for something I have done. I have heard my pastor say when he was a small boy he had stolen some darts and a toy car from the five-and-dime candy store. As an adult, God convicted him of this sin. Many years later he went back to the store, spoke to the store owner, and paid him back with interest for the candy he had stolen as a young boy.

The owner of the store asked, "Did you just get saved?" My pastor said yes and God was dealing with him on this small issue. So the money was paid back, he asked for forgiveness, the store owner smiled, and said yes, of course. My pastor needed to make all things right with everybody. He wanted nothing between him and God. He wanted nothing from his past to withhold blessing on his life, his family's life, or their future.

Think back on your life; think of all the incidents back to childhood or as an adult where we told a lie to gain an advantage in a particular situation. Most of the time lies were meaningless, and it would have been easier just to tell the truth. Or in the above example of stealing from a store even something very small, stealing is stealing in God's eyes. Little stealing habits follow people throughout their lives; the stealing just gets bigger and bigger as people get older and gain confidence on how to take things without paying for them.

We own a construction company that works in several states with multiple crews doing thousands of projects each year. How easy would it be for employees to be on the clock when they had stopped working? Stealing time for anyone is easy, whether in a factory on a production line or a high profile attorney billing for hours of work he never did. Lies and stealing, cheating in various forms in life are wrong in God's eyes. Confess to God when someone trusted you to be honest and you took advantage of them. This is the power of forgiveness through making things right before God.

Have you been hurt by someone or victimized by something in your past? Can you forgive someone who has hurt you so deeply? There is nothing in this world that will tell you or make you forgive someone. In an earlier chapter, I spoke about Holy Spirit telling me to forgive my robbers for what they had done like I have forgiven you. I will tell you with full honesty I did not respond well to that statement, not well at all. The Holy Spirit said to me again, forgive those men like I have forgiven you. Again I rejected the voice of the Holy Spirit.

I remember sitting back in my airplane seat and starting to think about forgiveness. How do you forgive someone for the hurt and trauma? I know the voice of the Holy Spirit, and I refused to give in. I continued to think about it, and think about it some more. Slowly I began to reason with myself, thinking why not, why should I? A feeling came over me that I cannot explain. Then I slowly said, "God I forgive those men for the hurt, trauma, and shame they brought me."

As I began to forgive and forgive more, thousands of pounds of weight were lifted off my shoulders. As the airplane ascended higher, God was showing me the power of forgiveness right there at thirty-thousand feet in the air.

I immediately felt the freedom after thirty-eight years of withholding forgiveness. I will tell you in all honestly I never knew I should have forgiven them. It was my right to be mad and angry at them for year after year of living in that bondage that was in all honestly holding me back to reaching my full potential.

I want all that God has for me and my family, I want everything—every spiritual gift, every blessing He has for every joy in life. I want it, just like my pastor said when he returned money for stolen items. That return with the store owner meant freedom from his past and freedom for his future. When God says something, just do it. Don't hold back; He has freedom from the past for you and freedom right now. Live it and believe it; it is yours and yours alone to have from this moment on.

The need to come clean on an issue or issues will help clear the conscience of the person who has hurt someone. The understanding of accepting responsibility for your actions and asking to be forgiven may be easy on superficial issues, but when you have hurt someone deeply, this becomes very difficult. How can I describe God's love for you? You can have your very best day or your very worst day; you can read your Bible eight hours a day or one minute a day — God simply loves you just the same.

Perhaps the same old nagging sin or temptation appears week after week, and while you say I'm not looking at that anymore, or I'm not going to do that anymore, you do it over and over again. You feel bad, and you feel foolish. Yet God forgets our mistakes just like it never even happened. Work hard to overcome a sinful nature, read your Bible, find a strong mentoring group, and attend a Bible preaching church that teaches God's word without compromise.

Starting from the beginning, ask, is my life right with God? Have I confessed my sins? Have I accepted Christ into my life? Do I have forgiveness for my salvation?

> Acts 13:38, ESV — "Let it be known to you therefore, brothers, that through this man forgiveness of sins is proclaimed to you..."

1 John 1:9, NIV — "If we confess our sins, he
is faithful and just and will forgive us our
sins and purify us from all unrighteousness."

The ultimate act of forgiveness is your salvation and
eternal life with the Father.

Let's look at this example: An easy way to start is to bring
it before God and say, "God I'm sorry I lied to my wife; I
have broken and violated my trust with her and within
our family." Starting with God begins the healing process.
God forgives when you are truly sorry, when you empty
yourself before Him and repent before Him, asking for
forgiveness for what you have done. This becomes sin
when you do wrong then ask for forgiveness as a pre-
planned action.

Later the husband tells the wife what he has done, tells
her he is sorry, and asks for her to forgive him. Her reac-
tion might be of hurt: how could you do this to me? I
trusted you, and you lied to me. Trust is broken, hearts
are broken, and she feels violated. After talking things
out she says, I forgive you.

This can take some time, a long time. Earlier in this book,
I wrote about after my robbery a little of the innocence
of mine is now gone. She may feel this way also; you're
forgiven, but the trust has been broken, and it takes time,
hard work, and counseling to rebuild trust.

The issues of forgiveness become much more complicated
than the example we just read about. How do you go
about forgiving someone who has hurt you so deeply
right down to your soul?

Proverbs 27:17, NIV—"As iron sharpens iron, so one person sharpens another."

Live to be healthy, go into the world and be a multiplier of forgiveness. Live to teach others, live to tell others your story of forgiveness. Declare, I am an overcomer, enrich others to live strong, and live intentionally, for a life well lived in Jesus Christ.

Establish new healthy relationships with healthy people. We previously read about choosing to be healthy. Look for support groups within churches such as counseling groups. A quick search will bring up multiple wellness groups in most metropolitan areas. Healthy people have a desire to be with healthy people; look for and find recommended groups in your area of need.

Most pastors have a network of business professionals that they can steer you into for needed help and counseling. Pastors can do counseling, and most churches today have a pastoral staff to help everything from teenagers to married couples to terminally sick people in hospitals and nursing homes. The pastors have been trained to be good listeners, and typically one of the first to offer help in time of need or crisis.

Pastors want to see people well and flourishing within their churches and communities. Pastors have limited time and training but are an excellent source of help; a meeting with a member of a pastoral staff will begin to determine the next steps that can be arranged.

There are two types of people: one type desires to be healthy to go on with their lives, to be a positive example to others around them, and the other type are wounded hurting people who love to live in their past hurts. This second type find others who will listen to them tell their stories over and over without any real commitment toward health and wholeness.

The type that desires to be healthy let their lives be lived in a way that shows Christ's work in their lives. Start being an overcomer — go and dig down deep into yourself and have the courage to change for the better. The courage to grow is certainly most difficult and is always difficult as is overcoming the pain of the past. And most important is the ability to forgive the people and the circumstances that have hurt you in the past.

The power of forgiveness is the key to ultimate freedom in every life. People who choose to forgive others recognize the hurts and feelings that must be dealt with. Most people hold that hurt deep inside themselves, hoping to forget the past. But as I have said before, the emotional hurts and scars are etched deep into the brain, just under the skin. Those memories can return on a moment's notice. Any number of circumstances can recall these memories in a second, sometimes triggered by something as innocent as a song on the radio.

Wounded people can learn from others that have overcome similar circumstances in their lives. Hearing a testimony from someone who has overcome abuse or been victimized by others is a ray of hope that they can be well, too. God is the God of comfort; He will comfort others through your story of healing and overcoming the hurts and abuse of your past.

As I have said before, misery loves company, and some people love to feel bad for themselves and draw in others to tell and retell their stories of past hurts and abuse. The previous statement is not meant to be insensitive — again, the hurts are real and cut clean to the bone — but to be well the focus needs to be on the future while working through the issues of the past.

Hurting people desire to be around healthy people. Healthy people desire to be around strong people. People tend to gravitate to stronger people in the groups. Leaders tend to be very strong people with clear direction in business and organizations. They are the ones who set the course and have the vision for the future.

Find someone who you can trust. Find a small group or counselor to speak with in complete confidence that nothing will be shared outside the group. Having someone gossip about sensitive issues might be as bad as the abuse or hurt itself; a break in confidence in a gossip scenario will further injure the hurting parties.

God does not want you to live a life of guilt and shame. That's why Jesus went to the cross to take away our hurt, our shame, and the mistakes we have made in our lives. God's message to us is love, to love ourselves in a healthy way free from the bondage and guilt of the past. The all-knowing, all-loving God the Father, Jesus Christ the Son, and the Holy Spirit want you to be healed and live a life of freedom to the fullest of your God-given potential.

> Ephesians 1:4, NIV — "For he chose us in him before the creation of the world to be holy and blameless in his sight..."

It is stated throughout the Bible how much God loves us. God chose us before the creation of the world, and nothing can separate you from His love. The only thing we need to do is receive His love, His wonderful all-encompassing love, acknowledging who God is and accepting Him as our Lord and Savior and asking for the forgiveness of your sins. This is the power of the cross and the power of forgiveness given to you and me: receive Jesus into your heart today — don't delay, do it — and begin this day in freedom from the past, and your new relationship in Christ.

Expect great things from God, for He is the God of healing, love, and forgiveness. He will enable you to do big things in your life, to live a life beyond your imagination and make all your dreams possible.

## CHAPTER 10 DISCUSSION QUESTIONS

> **LIFE LESSONS**
>
> Finding fresh strong people to be around is a benefit to moving forward. It takes the focus off myself to moving through issues as a group. Determining to live life with intention and with purpose to a limitless future.

## Points to Ponder

Small groups are an excellent way to be with others struggling with like issues. Learning to be a good listener is a key in the healing process. In a small group setting of trusting individuals do you listen or talk?

To effectively move on in the healing process it is good to verbalize the issues needing forgiveness; often times this brings the hurts to the surface. Do you like to tell your story? Why or why not?

Where are you in the forgiveness process with God, others and yourself?

# CHAPTER 11

# The Courage
# to Change

Matthew 18: 21–22, KJ2000 — "Then came Peter to him, and said, Lord, how often shall my brother sin against me, and I forgive him? Till seven times? Jesus said unto him, I say not unto you, Until seven times: but, Until seventy times seven."

*Memories run deep, but forgiveness runs deeper.*

I can replay the memories of the robbery night without thinking. If I'm going to be free, I'm going to need to change my way of thinking. I cannot simply default back in time and continue to dwell on the past memories and fears of that night. Nothing can change the past, which is now history, and the robbery is part of the story of my life. To change takes passion to live strong and make the necessary changes now for a better life and for a better future.

> Jeremiah 8:18, NIV — "You who are my Comforter in sorrow…"

I will call upon the Lord, and He is my comforter; He is my helper in time of need. It takes courage to forgive. I am saying, "No more will this control me." This is the line I draw in the sand, the boundary I have set forth: nothing comes into this space unless I choose to allow it.

To live in freedom will take lots of courage, the courage you might not even know you have. With God on your side, it is He and you; you are an army. Pray asking God for a hedge of protection from nightmares and bad memories of your past. Be determined to walk forth in victory. While you can't change the past, you can control your future. Be determined to stay strong one moment at a time to gain traction and strength walking in newfound self-confidence: say, from this moment, from this day, I will walk in victory over my past hurts and circumstances. With professional counseling and positive support groups, I will develop a plan of success for my future.

I cannot simply deny that this ever happened to me, but I choose to take control over this. It happened and I must accept this as a part of my past, but today I'm a new person in Jesus Christ.

> 2 Corinthians 5:17, KJB — "Therefore if any man *be* in Christ, he is a new creature: old things are passed away; behold, all things are become new."

The power of the enemy has been broken; today I refuse to live in the past any longer.

What Satan has meant for evil God will turn it for my good. Get victory over your past and use it to live a happy fulfilling life. And if you get the chance, promote your goodness into helping others. Our lives cannot be lived through the injustices of the past, but through the hope and healing in Jesus Christ.

> Ezra 10:4, NIV – "Rise up; this matter is in your hands. We will support you, so take courage and do it."

I pray for strength to not live in the past or visit the negative past events of my life. I pray that God delivers me from the pain and hardship of the memories of the past. This is hard and more difficult than it seems. Daily situations will flood my mind with things that make me uncomfortable. Walking alone in a parking ramp at night makes every hair on my body stand up. Maybe I have watched too many movies or is it my sensitivity on guard being in dark spaces due to the events of my past? I just avoid places like that altogether.

Big words are easier said than done. I have developed a daily routine of prayer asking God for protection, living forward and not backward, protecting my mind and my thought life to be a positive influence to those around me. Likewise, I cannot allow negative thoughts or negative people and memories to influence my future.

I can never allow people to bring up my past or continue to live back in the time where the pain and abuse originated from unless there is or will be a positive outcome from the conversation. Every relationship you have is either moving you closer to God, or pushing you further away from God.

My word in testimony of how God has healed me from the events of the past is a testimony in itself. God can use my testimony to bring hope and healing to others who can relate to similar events in their past, and for others to know God is good, that God cares about you and me. God will use my story to lift up others and to build their faith by hearing my testimony of God's faithfulness from the place of hurt to the place where I am today.

Healing is a choice. Choose to be a healthy person, set forth that today I am going to live in good health; mandate this before you get out of bed. Nothing can erase the hurts and abuse caused by others in my life. Diligently seek the medical help as needed to live in freedom. But today I can walk in victory because I am choosing to be strong. I will work at living forward and not looking or living back at my old life. Again, the events of my past are part of my life story; it is where I came from, but it will not define my future.

> Memories run deep, but forgiveness runs deeper.

The hurts and abuse that have victimized everyday people are infinite. The human mind cannot conceive the what and why people hurt each other.

There are times where people are just in the wrong place at the wrong time. I was one of those people. I was a happy-go-lucky sixteen-year-old boy working in a store late one summer evening. I happened to be the guy mopping up the floors instead of counting the cash going into the safe that night.

Why did Walt say, "Mike, clean up the floors" that night? Why not Jim? I had counted the cash many nights when the store closed. The outcome for Jim may have been completely different. Maybe the robbers would have abandoned the plan all together, or maybe Jim would have been killed.

I met Jesus that night during those forty-eight minutes of trauma. That meeting changed my life forever, and my testimony and my life have been fruitful for the kingdom.

Many people have come to Christ as He has used my life to share the gospel to others. Still maybe I was in the stockroom that night for this moment, writing a book on the power of forgiveness. A simple story that people can relate to, and find the freedom to forgive the ones who have hurt and abused you.

Today I desire to be well; I will live my life positively. I will not dwell on the past other than asking God to bless my day, to use my life to share my faith in a kind and respectful way. I ask to be delivered from harmful memories and to live life in a positive and healthy way, so my story could come out to help someone at any particular time. I almost never talk about it. I try daily to move on from it, but if God wants me to share it, I will.

> Jeremiah 29:11, NIV — "'For I know the plans I have for you,' declares the LORD, 'plans to prosper you and not to harm you, plans to give you hope and a future.'"

I cannot pretend it never happened. To pretend it never happened would be living in denial. My identity is not defined by the hurts and abuse of my past; my identity is in my Lord and Savior Jesus Christ, and my life in Christ tells me I have a future free from the bondage and hurts from the past. I have a future, and the word says, what Satan meant for your harm both in the moments of hurts and abuse, God intends for good. The Bible promises hope and healing and a future. Live it, grab onto it, and walk it out today, declaring, I have a future ahead of me, a future of wholeness and completeness in Jesus Christ.

My life as I live it demands truth, that I live by truth, that I speak the truth, and that I act in a truthful and honorable way. This is the standard I hold myself and my family too.

My faith demands the truth. Without truth, it leaves huge cracks and holes in my character and integrity. God has called me to speak the truth and live honorability in my faith walk. With caution, I will speak about my robbery. I have found that it's okay to visit the past, but I don't let it take up residence.

Earlier in this book, I spoke about trying to find the robbers' names, to introduce myself to them, to tell them about my faith, and to tell them I have forgiven them. On the surface, this seemed like a great idea, and I did try to find out who they were. But I was having no success. I spoke to friends who might know them, but they couldn't remember any names or other details. After weeks of doing research and internet searches, I simply gave up.

Too much time and research began to bog me down, and emotionally it was far too taxing on me. Without realizing it I began to dwell the facts and slowly began to live back there; it was starting to consume me. I quickly realized that if God would have me meet them, He would re-introduce us. I left this in God's hands, for they are His children, and I have moved on, not out of not caring, just out of my own mental health and emotional well-being.

Healing is a journey. Develop a sense or a feeling when you are being steered off course. Most people have a story about difficulty in their lives, and they are willing to tell anybody who will listen. I am a loving and caring person, and I will listen to someone's story, but when the story shifts to dominating self-centeredness and angrily bashing the other person or other people, I back away. It's there you can tell if that person is working toward wellness and finding forgiveness or if they are an angry bitter person out to slam and run others down for their own personal satisfaction.

The most difficult people always have some negative things to say about an ex-spouse. The fact is they are your ex-spouse and something happened so that you and they do not get along—that's why you're not married anymore. It takes a big person to forgive an ex-spouse; the list of wrongs can go on forever.

Cheating, gambling, drinking, drugs, money, laziness, physical abuse, and many other things can be part of the list. The love of materialism, excessively working to keep up and provide for all those wants and desires can be on the list. Meanwhile couples can quickly grow apart trying to make ends meet, and the lack of money is one of the leading causes of divorce today.

Today's prisons are filled with prisoners because they were victims of abuse or neglect. Hurting people hurt other people. Each and every person in this world needs love and forgiveness. We are human beings, and human beings make mistakes. Some mistakes are so large they are almost unforgivable to the human intellect, but we serve a big God, the God of possibilities who makes all things right. To find forgiveness in the most difficult circumstances is a modern-day miracle. The road to forgiveness begins with the courage to change.

## CHAPTER 11 DISCUSSION QUESTIONS

> **LIFE LESSONS**
>
> It takes an amazing amount of courage to change. If we decide to live in the past circumstance our life will never progress to its full potential. The courage to change is personal. To grow you need to change no matter how hard it is.

### Points to Ponder

Do I have the courage to accept the responsibilities of my past?

The concept of intentional living comes by way of living life with a plan and purpose, without a plan permanent change is difficult. Do you want to change?

Acceptance of your mistakes is the first step in living a responsible life; excuses never carry the weight of truth.

To live your life in truth you must take a hard look at your integrity to determine if any cracks exist, and if there are cracks, to work hard to repair them. Do I live my life in truth?

# CHAPTER 12

# Forgiveness is a Process

Ephesians 4:32, NASB—"Be kind to one another, tender-hearted, forgiving each other, just as God in Christ also has forgiven you."

*In the midst of your incredible hurts, loss, and pain, may our God of peace and comfort wrap His arms of love around you throughout the storm.*

Forty-two years ago I started out on a journey as a sixteen-year-old working a summer job at a local grocery store. That night ended in near tragedy for me, nearly getting killed. The physical harm was over the next day, but the emotional scars lived on for decades. The process for my forgiveness took me on a thirty-eight-year journey before I could come to terms with my robbers. My robbers may have never thought about that night again, and that's okay, for in my heart I have forgiven them and the slate has been wiped clean.

> Matthew 16:24, KJB – "Then Jesus said unto
> his disciples, if any *man* will come after me,
> let him deny himself, and take up his cross,
> and follow me."

Some years ago I met some dear friends, Pastor Moses
and his wife Diane. Pastor Moses and Diane minister in
an inner city church in Grand Rapids, Michigan. Moses
has done this for over eighteen years. I am proud to call
Moses and Diane my friends.

God has called them to minister to everyday hurting
people. Moses retired from his secular job two years ago.
Year after year Moses went to work and then came home
tired each day. When most of us need our weekends
for rest and recreation, Moses and Diane went to work
ministering to the inner city people without any pay or
compensation.

Moses and Diane are following what God has for them.
As a couple, they make disciples out of everyday people.
They are people after God's heart, and most importantly,
they love people right where they are in life.

Moses and Diane passionately lead the church with
everything they have. Loving the hurting people of
Grand Rapids was and is on their hearts today. They
teach the Bible to anybody who walks through the door.
The church has a vibrant ministry to common people
from all walks of life.

When I began to write this book, the people from Moses'
church were always on my mind. The faces in the congregation are like any other church: the faces of single
mothers with arms wrapped around innocent children,

mothers worried about their future. But for now they are in God's house, and all is right, and they are safe. The look of others is that of people who are over-comers, some people that have made mistakes in their past, and others who are still in the process of moving forward. The key to overcoming your past mistakes is imbedded in forgiveness, living forward and not looking back at the past.

This is where the rubber meets the road in ministry. If everybody was whole and healed nobody would need Jesus, and they could go on living their lives on their own terms. Pastor Moses and Diane are exactly where God wants them and is using them to teach and love the people in their community. The church has a vibrant meals program. In its first year, thousands of people have been fed meals along with a faith-based message. Moses says, "Food brings people out, so while they are here we feed them, love them, and bless them in God's word."

Moses and Diane are originally from New Jersey. Both had grown up in Christian homes, but through some bad and difficult choices, they began to run with the wrong crowd. The crowd influenced them into the partying life where drugs and alcohol became their lifestyle. Their lives started a deep spiral downward. Then God did an amazing thing: He first spoke to Diane and then to Moses to stop living this lifestyle. God delivered them instantly from their addictions. They cleaned up their lives and turned their lives over to God to serve Him with their whole hearts.

In the past, Moses and Diane have walked in the shoes of the people of the inner city. Drug and alcohol problems are not limited to the inner city neighborhoods though. Moses sees it as a cultural problem that has reached each and every American town and neighborhood and crosses every social demographic and economic line from successful businessmen to the homeless people on the street.

There is a special connection when you meet people in life whose lives represent experience. They have walked the walk and now speak of the goodness of God's love and faithfulness. It is through lonely and difficult times when we are stretched in the heat of the battle that we grow and develop in our Christ-like character.

Moses and Diane can speak to people from an experienced point of view. They have lived life in some of the difficulties of life's challenges, and this gives their ministry the realism and vitality to connect to everyday people. When pastors' lives reflect realism and some real road time, their message often is easily relatable to the congregation.

Pastor Moses and Diane's life was met with tragedy a few years ago when their thirty-eight-year-old daughter died suddenly from a heart attack. This left three grandchildren that needed a home. Moses and Diane now assumed the roles of parents and grandparents to these three teenage children. Some people ask, "Why, why God, what's the sense in this?" Moses and Diane chose to stay busy with their grandchildren and grieve their loss together as a family. It won't do anybody any good to sit and feel sorry for themselves.

Moses says with a smile, "My grandchildren will continue being raised in a Christian home." Through the difficulties of the loss of their daughter, they still are the steady rock in these children's lives. These days find them getting kids off to school and attending school conferences along with their other church duties and responsibilities. Many grandparents find themselves raising their grandchildren today. Diane said they wouldn't have it any other way.

About one year after their daughter died, they received a call from New Jersey informing them that their granddaughter was very sick. She soon passed away at the age of nineteen from a heart aneurysm. The grip of grief soon took hold again. Once again they needed to feel God's presence in their lives. They knew God is good all the time, but sometimes it's just hard to understand when you are in the heat of the battle, trial, or circumstance.

On a recent summer morning, my wife and I were cleaning the garage, and Moses stopped by to pick up some fish we had for his congregation. We took a break and sat down in our sunroom and began to discuss Moses' family reunion trip out West while drinking some tea. My wife made our tea. For the first time in over twenty years, Moses contentedly sipped his tea without adding any sugar; God had delivered him from sugar at that moment—in an instant. Moses said it just happened—it's a God thing. To the believer, God is always at work in our lives.

As we talked, Moses was excited and happy to be taking his wife Diane, his children, and grandchildren out West. He would preach at his family gathering to about seventy-five relatives, many he has not seen in many years. All of his grandchildren were going on the vacation except for Seth who was not living by all the rules of the house. Moses said Seth chose to not go on the family vacation but stayed behind to work at his job. Moses felt Seth was a typical eighteen-year-old boy, expressing his independence.

Moses and Diane live on an income that Diane provides from her job and the Social Security that Moses receives. Moses said, "There has been little or no going out for any kind of dinners—just home cooking to save money. We have saved for eighteen months to be able to take this vacation." I could see the excitement in his eyes knowing his bags were packed and their flight was leaving in three or four hours.

Our conversation shifted from Moses' vacation plans to my current project. I spoke to Moses about this book project *The Power of Forgiveness*. He listened as I told him the robbery story, the trauma of being tied up, locked in a cooler, and so on. I spoke to Moses about all the years of carrying anger toward these men who hurt me and how God spoke to me on a plane at thirty-thousand feet saying, "Forgive these men as I have forgiven you." I told him I did not want to forgive these guys but would rather stay angry at them. Then my heart softened, I sat back in my seat, and I forgave the men who hurt me. The plane lifted off the ground and a thousand pounds lifted off my shoulders. The change of heart I had and the feeling of letting go all the pressure of that night was now in God's hands and laid at the foot of the cross.

Moses listened, encouraged me to continue writing, and then commented on how the book would free the readers from hurt or abuse and lead people to Christ through salvation. Listening with deep conviction in his heart, Moses said it was like God was speaking to him about something to prepare him for the future. He continued to think and ponder about the power of forgiveness and a feeling came over Moses like a slight restless spirit.

Saying our goodbyes, we wished him well on his trip, hoping he would enjoy himself and get some rest with family. Moses drove out the driveway with not a clue of what was about to happen to him and his family in the days ahead.

Moses and Diane boarded their flight in Grand Rapids for the three-and-a-half-hour flight out West. During the flight, Moses spoke to Diane about our meeting and the book I was working on about forgiveness. Everything was good as they landed later that night and were greeted by relatives at the airport.

A couple of days later their grandson Seth and his girlfriend were out for a walk near downtown Holland with friends and Seth's dad. A beautiful Michigan summer evening soon turned to tragedy as they were walking to a gas station to get some snacks and soda.

Seth and his girlfriend waited outside the gas station while the others went in to purchase the snacks. A car drove by and someone in the car yelled out a remark to Seth's girlfriend. Seth took offense to the comment as the car slowed and then stopped at the curb ahead.

The time was nearing 10 PM when a girl and a couple of guys jumped out of the car and walked up to Seth. Soon their voices raised, and the men began to push at Seth. Seth was alone and defenseless. Seth was defending his girlfriend's honor against the words that were spoken to her from the car as it passed.

Daylight was turning into darkness as the words became more heated. One of the men lunged at Seth, and in less than a second, the man stabbed Seth right in the heart.

With one swipe of the knife blade, one stab wound, Seth collapsed to the ground and was dead in a few seconds. The others ran away like cowards as Seth's girlfriend cried for help. Seth's dad then exited the gas station to find his son lying dead on the concrete sidewalk, where he had left him one or two minutes before.

> In the midst of your incredible hurts, loss, and pain, may our God of peace and comfort wrap His arms of love around you throughout the storm.

Within minutes, Moses and Diane received the call that Seth, their only grandson, had been stabbed and was now dead. Now thousands of miles away, Moses and Diane tried to make sense of the news. Most times when we receive difficult news the shock is too much to take; the news is unbelievable until the reality starts to set in. The family gathers and prays for peace in their hearts, that the killer or killers are found and quickly brought to justice.

Moses and Diane might think they were they too hard on Seth, leaving him home while the family left for vacation. If he had gone with them, he might still be alive. Some difficult decisions are met with eternal consequences. Moses did the right thing by having a disciplined home and an example for the other children in the home to follow.

Seth was a creative young man. He not only taught himself to play the guitar and sing but he was also incredibly talented at drawing and artistry too. His imagination to paint pictures or create things was a gift from God. Seth was in the wrong place at the wrong time. The car that drove by that night was looking for trouble and found it. A joyride for some young kids that night ended in the tragedy of a young eighteen-year-old's life that was full of promise and dreams yet to be fulfilled. That night, if it wasn't Seth, it might have been another innocent victim along life's way.

Like Seth, many people are just in the wrong place at the wrong time. It happened to me working in a grocery store late one night. With every tragedy, we are faced with the choice to forgive or not to forgive. Moses and Diane want to see justice served on the young man who killed their only grandson. Justice will always be served in time; people can avoid the law only for so long. Ultimately each and every one of us will stand before the God of the universe and be judged for our actions.

Moses and Diane came to my office a few days later. We closed the door and along with my wife we all prayed together. The hurt and brokenness of their hearts was more than one could bear. We prayed for peace as Seth's funeral was being planned and that God would move in the funeral service. We especially prayed for the young people in the crowd that they would know how fragile life is and how ever so quickly life can change with eternity in the balance.

The stories of violence are played out every day on the streets of America; however, this time it was personal, not just another story on the news. Like the other victims of senseless crime and violence, this young man was a son, a brother, a friend, and a grandson. A life full of promise ended in a moment of anger.

> Mark 11:26, KJB — "But if ye do not forgive, neither will your Father which is in heaven forgive your trespasses."

Moses looked at me with tear-filled eyes. He said, "I know I have to forgive the man who killed my grandson. Mike, it's going to be hard to do that." He paused and then added, "Just like you forgave your robbers in your story, we will forgive my grandson's killer."

With the pain of the loss of their grandson's life, the grieving process is something they must go through step by step. The forgiveness process will be an intentional act from their hearts. Forgiving the man who killed their grandson is a step-by-step process as God takes away and lifts the burden from anger and bitterness to peace and freedom. Anger and bitterness will never bring Seth back, but as the healing process begins, peace and joy will return in their hearts.

It is only natural that Moses and Diane would be angry and resentful; however, they are believers and teachers of the Word of God, and they will work to be different. They are committed to the forgiveness and healing process. Moses and Diane will carry the torch, leading by example, ministering to their family first and then to the church congregation. We are all hurting people in different ways and for different reasons.

As pastors of their church, Moses and Diane know about forgiveness and what the Bible says about forgiveness. "But this is hard," he said, "We will forgive over time, but our hope is that justice is served in a swift way and that the man responsible will be held accountable."

> Psalms 51:10, KJB — "Create in me a clean heart, O God; and renew a right spirit within me."

The killer will also stand before God for his actions on that summer night. What will he say? We are all guilty of sin and mistakes we have made throughout our lives. Very few people will stand before God for murdering someone, but we're all guilty of something. Forgiveness starts with you and God, when you get your heart right with Him. After that, He will work with you on the other people or situations and circumstances in your life where and when forgiveness needs to take place.

Moses and Diane are on the forgiveness journey that took me thirty-eight years to complete. I suspect forgiveness will come much quicker for them because they know finding forgiveness will energize them and bring forth the freedom in Christ that Jesus offers to everyone.

Moses and Diane left one summer day, traveling on vacation meeting with family and friends. Their trip was marked with tragedy, having lost their first and only grandson on the streets of Holland, Michigan that July night. Moses and Diane never asked for their lives to change. If they could, they would go back and change things, but life doesn't work that way. Moses and Diane will walk out the days ahead, step-by-step on their journey of forgiveness.

Then, my friends, their lives will be filled once again with peace and joy. Moses and Diane are walking out these days one day at a time. Then, as they have taught others, they will come to understand the total and complete power of forgiveness in their lives, forgiving the young man who has caused so much pain and heartache for taking the life of their only grandson.

Moses and Diane are walking out these steps as I write this tonight. Glimpses of hope of the future, smaller amounts of grief today, a little more healing, a little more peace and comfort. God is here in the hurt, God is here in the despair, and He can fulfill the need.

## CHAPTER 12 DISCUSSION QUESTIONS

> ### LIFE LESSONS
>
> Forgiveness is a process. This chapter speaks to the hurting hearts of Moses and Diane and their family. Our faith teaches us to forgive others even when it hurts. Forgiveness can happen all at once or as a process, but the important thing to remember is to forgive. Without forgiveness, anger and bitterness will take hold of your heart. The sooner the forgiveness process begins, the sooner your healing will begin.

### Points to Ponder

The hurt and pain that Moses and Diane felt when their only grandson was murdered is beyond human understanding. Explain times when you forgave someone who hurt you deeply.

Was forgiveness a process, or were you simply able forgive and forget?

Being angry and getting even are the world's way of dealing with pain; how is God's plan different from the world's?

Why is forgiveness more beneficial than revenge?

Forgiveness is a process; write down your process on how you have forgiven someone.

# CHAPTER 13

# My Healing Process

Psalm 37:5, KJ2000 — "Commit your way to the LORD, trust also in him, and he shall bring it to pass."

*God, you rescued me, you called me your own, through my hardship you have given me a greater purpose in my life, to live for you and to serve others.*

As I spoke in the chapter "The Robbery", I can say I was brought up in a Christian home. Our family faith was deep in the Methodist faith, and I am ever grateful to my parents for taking me and my siblings to church. Those early years are deeply imbedded into my memory. Sunday mornings would find us boys polishing our shoes, dressing in nice clothing, and of course attaching our clip-on ties. As a family, we loaded into our car for the couple mile ride to church.

We sat as a family with the exception of our dad who sang in the choir. Dad towered over the rest of the choir standing 6 foot 5 inches tall while he sang. I can remember how much he cared; I can remember seeing the sense of pride on his face as he sang. This also gave dad an excellent view of his family. The look in his eyes from the choir loft was enough to set you straight because we boys were always misbehaving.

We had a good grounding in the Lord and in our faith. As time went on, we knew about God, but He seemed a million miles away. We prayed at dinners, but it didn't go much deeper than that.

There are times in life where we are confronted with God, sometimes in extreme circumstances that are wake-up calls, like an unexpected death of someone close to us, a near miss accident or illness, or an out-of-the-blue situation like a robbery.

To know God, to truly know the God of the universe, moves us from the near-miss types of situations to the closeness of our relationship we have with Him. This is where my life shifted from the God that's a million miles away to the precious God the Father, Jesus the Son, and the Holy Spirit in my heart. As we read in the robbery chapter, my life hung in the balance for forty-eight minutes, twenty of those minutes with a knife blade pressed against my throat and my spine.

It was then I learned how to pray, and pray I did. There was nothing else I could do. Looking back today I am glad for it. God got my attention quickly. At times I have heard some people say in a moment of crisis, there's nothing else we can do now; let's pray. My prayer life changed my way of thinking and took my life on an ever-changing journey in the days, weeks, and years ahead.

My God is ever present, He is always with me, so that today I pray about everything in my life.

He is almighty God, everlasting Father and wonderful counselor to me every day of my life, all the time.

The previous paragraph speaks about our human will, our wanting to have control over all the options. We're human; that's how we are programmed to think. The believer's heart understands that God knows everything; there are no surprises to Him. So many years ago I shifted from me to Him, and I began to give God my will and my life and placed it into His hands, submitting myself to Him, allowing Him to do a work in my life and through my life, however He decided to do it.

Part of my healing process was to intentionally leave the past behind — the memories of the knives, the ropes that tied my hands behind my back, the look in the robbers' eyes, the look of pure evil that my life didn't matter to them if I lived or died that day. I was a bother to them, someone who just got in the way to their money for drugs. I lived because God protected me and has a plan and a purpose for my life. I am grateful that my life was spared that day.

Little by little I could see where doors were opening and doors would close when making critical decisions. My prayer life deepened, and my relationship with the Lord continues to be more intimate. I ask God for His closeness, that I would hear His voice, that I would have a greater understanding for my life and its impact on others. My life has become very intentional, living life on purpose for others.

Part of my healing process is my investing in my relationship with the Lord. A simple and basic Christian principle is we can never do enough to win God's love for us. God loves us more than we can ever imagine. No amount of giving, serving, or working for the Lord makes Him love us any more or any less than He already does. His love can never be earned; it is a free gift for us that His love was given on the cross the day He died for us and for our sins.

My investing into God's kingdom is through prayer and reading, gaining knowledge either through reading the Bible or the other ten or twelve books I read and study every day. The knowledge through what I have learned allows me to help others that are hurting. This study has taught me to be a good listener, and if appropriate, give comments to others that are helpful in our discussions. At times it might be tempting to shoot off answers and be the answer guy, but it's much better to a good listener and speak only when necessary or when asked.

I also live by investing into the lives of others. I have led fundraising efforts for special projects, worked on various ministries leading volunteer groups to serve others. I enjoy the meat-and-potatoes parts of ministry, specifically feeding people, caring for and counseling people, helping make their homes and neighborhoods better and safer places to live. Some people have been so beaten down by life not only in the inner city but everywhere from all walks of life they just can hardly put one foot in front of another.

People need hope, and they need someone to listen. These are perfect times to share our faith while building someone up and giving them a hand. The healing for me is while helping others, what better time for me to get my thoughts off myself while pouring God's love into others? This is no feel-good-about-myself ministry; it is about truly loving and caring about people and seeing them succeed at whatever level they are.

> God, you rescued me, you called me your own, through my hardship you have given me a greater purpose in my life, to live for you and to serve others.

My vision goes from looking at myself and memories of the past toward investing into people, sharing my faith, and building them up to be the best that they can be. So as my vision is about helping others, my healing continues to take place in my life. Any time my focus is on others and not on my past, others win, and I especially win by taking one more step forward in life.

It is amazing to pour God's love into people and see the instant results in their eyes. People receive love and understand love if it is given from the heart with no strings attached. We shouldn't feed addictions or further their addictions, but through love and counseling, real progress can be made, where lives can change from a life of prostitution to a life of self-worth and self-sufficiency. The power of forgiveness gives life to the hopeless that is a life full of hope, to lives being changed as God directs them to their future.

If we give to others without expecting anything in return or to expect quickly measured results, the possibilities are endless to what God can do. Plain and simple, taking my eyes off myself and giving to others has incredible healing power for me.

One of the most important parts of my healing is I have sought help when I needed to talk to someone, normally for myself with a friend or a brother over a cup of coffee to bounce around a few ideas. Trusted valued friends are worth all the money in the world when you need to talk.

The other side is walking on my farm or plowing a field and pondering the issues when I have concerns. Nothing beats sitting in a tree stand with God. A pastor once told me there is no greater place to be than out on a limb with God. It's a place where you are with Him; there is nothing distracting you, just a heart-to-heart talk with the God almighty the creator. God has spoken to me about some really big decisions that I needed to make, all the while enjoying my time with Him.

My brother and I named one of our tree stand locations the pothole. It's named that because it sits overlooking a low depression in the land full of tall weeds and thick underbrush.

One particular morning while sitting in this stand, I received the news that my friend Brent just passed away at the age of thirty-eight from a heart attack. He died on Christmas Eve leaving two small boys and a loving wife Jamie behind. My heart sank like from a low blow to the gut; I was in shock from the news. I went to God right then and there for his wife and children.

Another time in the pothole tree stand, God put on my heart to work with an inner city ministry group my friends Greg and his wife Leah were starting. With the help of about twenty volunteers, we provided about thirty Christmas meals for an inner city neighborhood.

The money was supplied, the ladies shopped for turkeys, sweet potatoes, stuffing, other fixings, and pies for dessert.

Early on a cold December Michigan morning, we split into teams delivering the boxes of meals. We also included an adult and children's daily devotionals and prayed with each family that received the food. It is a joy that my wife and I have been able to partner with this dynamic couple in their ministry in the inner city streets of Grand Rapids, Michigan.

Greg and Leah lead their group of volunteers and continue to work with the neighborhood weekly, investing into the families. The neighborhood has a new sense of pride where lives are being changed, the crime rate is going down, and people care once again about their neighbors and their community. Through their efforts, individual lives and families have found forgiveness and a new hope in Jesus Christ. Greg and Leah love on families, asking for nothing in return. Today that neighborhood is an example of what can happen when you share, love, and care for people right where they are.

Years earlier God put an idea in my wife's heart about starting our own business, I was truly nervous to take this leap of faith, leaving the security of a regular paycheck, family insurance coverage, and so on. We prayed together, the doors opened, and we started our little business with one employee.

Years have passed, and the company has flourished through the good times and down times as the economy has floated in and out of recessions and political changes. Laying off hard-working talented people is one of the hardest things in business. It teaches us to be lean and careful no matter how good things appear.

We believe owning a business is an extension of our ministry. We give jobs and train people to learn necessary skills to give them opportunity. As they develop their skills, we empower them to become leaders in our company and in their personal lives in our community.

We prayed for direction how to do things differently, and reinventing the wheel more times than you could imagine, working hard to create value with our customers so that when work would be available, they would choose us over our competitors' companies. We prayed for the favor of God on our lives and the lives of our employees. We kept going, and it was hard; there were times when things were very uncertain but the work always came through.

Today our construction company is a nationally recognized brand, owned by my wife, my brother, and me. Today we work with some of the world's largest companies solving their problems through creative thinking and solutions. Our company today is led by some incredibly gifted and intelligent people that understand submitting to our customers' needs allows us to better serve our customers, and our companies work well together for our future.

My life is a work in process; my healing will be a lifetime effort of overcoming the post-traumatic stress (PTS) from the past. Everybody that has been a victim of hurts and abuse needs to find the path of healing for themselves. My life is an example of the possibilities that can take place by living a life with intentionality for a purpose.

The reality for my healing can be summed up in a few thoughts.

I am grateful for the love and protection God the Father, Jesus the Son, and the Holy Spirit showed me on the robbery night, and every night since. What I experienced that night from fear to finding my faith in God, turned my life around, I am thankful, so eternally thankful, for my walk with Christ. I confess that I am not perfect and can still make mistakes. Today I walk as a new person in Jesus Christ, looking forward and not back.

I have chosen to live forward; I have decided to not live back where and when the crimes against me took place. To live back there is counterproductive to moving forward in my life. I choose to live by this strong statement of faith and purpose for my life. The rehashing of the night's events do nothing for my future unless the story of my testimony surviving that night bring people closer to God and help them overcome the pain of abuse or being a victimized at the hands of others or any other unfortunate event in their lives!

I have purposely chosen to take the focus off myself, removing the thoughts and worries of yesterday, living today with God's promise, and knowing that it holds a million possibilities wherever the Holy Spirit leads me. My healing in part is in sowing seeds of hope into the lives of others, serving others so that they can live a life made good in Jesus Christ, a life full of goodness and opportunity.

# CHAPTER 13 DISCUSSION QUESTIONS

---

### LIFE LESSONS

My healing process was a deliberate act of my will. When I accepted Jesus into my heart, my heart changed. I chose to read my Bible and to pray everyday. I wanted my relationship with God the Father to be all in. I wanted to grow and develop in my faith walk by living intentionally.

---

## Points to Ponder

Are you living and growing as a believer? If not what's holding you back?

One of the greatest joys is in volunteering and serving others. Do you invest into the lives of others? Why or why not?

Are you living life with an intentional purpose? What does that mean to you?

# CHAPTER 14

# Thankfulness and Gratitude

Colossians 2:7, NIV—"...in him, strengthened in the faith as you were taught, and overflowing with thankfulness."

*Give God twenty-four hours, He can change every circumstance in your world; now trust Him to do it.*

My encounter with the robbers changed my life many years ago. I was at that time a very happy sixteen-year-old young man enjoying everything that life had to offer, and then in a moment, my innocence was gone forever.

I had a great relationship with my dad; we did everything from household projects to hunting and fishing together. As most guys I had a small group of close friends that I hung out with, but my time with my dad was special. I am grateful for my parents who gave us the gift of their time.

Some of the best memories with my dad were times we would drive up north to go trout fishing on the Baldwin

River. We would leave early in the morning about 4:30 AM. Our drive would take about an hour and a half; as a teenager I would sleep most of the way. Reaching our destination, it would just be getting light, Dad had his favorite spots, and I had mine; we would arrange to meet at the railroad bridge later in the morning.

Meeting at the railroad bridge is rich in our family history. My dad met up with his dad there. I would have loved to hear the conversations between my dad and my grandfather. I would also meet with my brothers Steve and Phil to discuss the ones we caught and the ones that got away.

This next year I plan to fish with my grandson, Kaemin and sons, Mike Jr. and youngest son Matthew at that very spot.

Dad was a fishing master; he caught fish when everyone else couldn't get a bite.

We would throw our lines in and talk about how we fished earlier spots and look at the trout we had caught, telling each of the stories as we now waited for the fish to bite. Little did I know how important those times were; they are some of the best memories I have with him.

It's hard to describe the pleasure of sitting side by side with my dad fishing; sometimes not a word being said for an hour or two. These were sacred times spent together. I'm very thankful that we cleared our schedules and took the time to fish because my dad died from cancer a few years later when I was twenty years old. Words cannot describe how much I miss that man. I am so very thankful for the time we had together.

There are two types of people in this world. Those who are thankful and those who are not. Thankful and grateful people have a more optimistic outlook on life. They are looking on the brighter side of things, and for the good things in life.

Thankfulness breeds an optimistic attitude in life, and an optimistic attitude opens the door to forgiveness, and for-giveness leads to personal freedom in your life. Thankful people are happy pleasant people and other people want to be around happy people.

When my dad became sick with terminal cancer, I had an overwhelming sense of loss when he died, not just because my father died, but because I lost a very close friend. I wish everyone could have the kind of relation-ship my dad and I had—very close and personal.

It is easy for me to be thankful and grateful for that was how I was raised. Though we were not a perfect family by any means, we were together, we were loved, and that's what mattered. I do not have to look too far back to see how blessed we were as I hear stories of less-than-per-fect parents.

I have heard hundreds of stories of moms and dads who drank and drank heavily. The enormous toll this placed on the families goes without saying. A lot of dads drank themselves into drunkenness, and then things often turned violent.

The violence rears its ugly head in many forms, most of the times with the mother being thrown around or beaten up in front of the children; when dad was done with mom, he then looked for the kids to either beat on or exercise his domination over them. There are countless stories of small boys and girls that may have been touched, their bodies trespassed on by alcoholic fathers or others relatives.

Forgiveness comes hard to a child of an abusive parent; the abuse comes in many ways too numerous to even try to mention. Most abuse happens night after night and goes on year after year, while another trusting adult stands by and says nothing and does nothing to protect the child.

This can be viewed as double abuse to the child where parents continue to either cover for the other parent or do not speak up for fear of making a family scene. The children live in constant fear of the unknown or the known behaviors of the times before.

My heart goes out to hurting children; in fact, my hearts aches for all hurting people who were often victims of hurt and child abuse when they were young. Some of the stories I have heard of abused children are very difficult to even understand. Where does the happiness and joy come from these damaged lives, and how can they let go of their past?

> Philemon 1:6, NLT—"And I am praying that you will put into action the generosity that comes from your faith as you understand and experience all the good things we have in Christ."

## Thankful for Opportunities to Share Our Faith

I am thankful for the opportunities to share my faith, for they are encounters with eternity, hearing the voice of the Holy Spirit, speaking with love and respect. Some people share the word and some lead people to Christ. Be ready, then listen to others; be prepared for a word in season.

> Give God twenty-four hours, He can change every circumstance in your world; now trust Him to do it.

Another growing aspect of child abuse are the mothers who drink alcohol or abuse drugs during their pregnancies and received little or no prenatal care. I was volunteering at an inner city ministry block party one summer afternoon where I met a young lady named Mary, who was about seven-and-one-half months pregnant at the time. Mary was smoking cigarettes while we shared some conversation; her face beamed as she spoke about her upcoming birth of her child.

As we moved deeper into the conversation she revealed during her entire pregnancy she was working in prostitution continuing to have multiple unprotected sexual encounters daily. Mary lived off the public assistance system and what little money her pimp would give her, there were times Mary traded sexual favors for several types of hard drugs.

I along with a few others continued to talk with Mary about her life and the things that God can do. Mary continued to listen and ask questions. We tried our best to show her proper housing and counseling services that would fit her situation as well as a couple of local churches.

> Ezekiel 22:30, JB2000 — "And I sought for a
> man among them that should make up the
> hedge and stand in the gap before me for
> the land that I should not destroy it, but I
> found no one.

In the end, we prayed with Mary a prayer of salvation, and she received Jesus Christ into her life. Mary's baby would most likely be born into this world being addicted to drugs.

Mary chose to do no prenatal care exams up to this point in her pregnancy, so her baby might be born with developmental issues due to Mary's drug abuse. Our time came to a close, and Mary refused all our offers of help and services that could be supplied to her. Sadly, Mary walked away, met up with her group of friends, lit another cigarette, and walked toward the streets.

Mary's story is a reality in some parts of our culture; though rare, some children are born into this world under those circumstances. My hope and prayer is that Mary turned her life around and is making good choices for her and her child. Like Mary we have all made mistakes, but there is time to turn your life around, and there is still time to make things right. Thankfully we serve a God of second chances.

> Ephesians 3:17, NLT — "Then Christ will
> make his home in your hearts as you trust
> in him. Your roots will grow down into
> God's love and keep you strong."

Our God is an awesome God, and He loves us no matter where we are in life, and no matter what we have done.

His love, that all-encompassing love, doesn't cost a thing. No matter the scholar that has several college degrees or the person with no education and is homeless on the streets, God loves everyone just the same. That love cannot be earned by working for Him or by being a good person. This love is a free gift for everyone to have; they just have to ask Jesus into their hearts and ask for their sins to be forgiven.

Today I live a life of thankfulness most likely because that was how I was raised. My childhood was that of middle-income family with no frills, just the basics in life. When we received something, it was special and we were thankful; my parents had little money to spend on extra things. My parents gave us their time like going on picnics, camping, and other low-cost actives.

Families today don't need super parents; instead, families need to be connected through listening, talking, and communicating with one another — no distractions just paying attention to one another and caring for one another.

So the story of life is that some people are born into privilege while others are born into poverty, but one day we will stand before God the Father, and He will ask did I know you?

# CHAPTER 14 DISCUSSION QUESTIONS

> **LIFE LESSONS**
>
> Despite some difficult times in my life I am choosing to live my life with gratefulness and thankfulness. Gratefulness is a byproduct of my faith. I have learned that to live life less than thankful is a poor example of who I am choosing to be, and a poor example of my faith walk. I choose to be a happy person and for that I am thankful.

Points to Ponder

If you could pick a particular time either now or at a time in the past when you were the most happy, what activities were you doing?

List the top ten things in your life that you are most thankful for.

Do you live a life of thankfulness? Why or why not?

What are your best memories?

# CHAPTER 15

# How Big Is Your God?

John 17:3, NIV — "Now this is eternal life:
that they may know you, the only true God,
and Jesus Christ, whom you have sent."

*The day will come when every knee will bow and
every tongue confess that Jesus Christ is Lord.*

In the heat of the robbery moment, I chose to meet God
quickly. I had no formal thoughts; rather, something
deep inside of me told me my heart was not right with
God, and I knew it was true. While the robbers were
shouting orders in my ears, I heard the loving voice of
God the Father saying, "Come to me and I will protect
you; I will keep you from danger and harm."

In the moments that followed, I was barely able to orga-
nize my thoughts. However, I did respond by asking God
to forgive me for my mistakes and promised to serve Him
forever if He got me out of this. It was nothing fancy and
really nothing formal. I simply cried out to God, and He
heard my plea and answered my prayer. I consider this

moment to be my moment of salvation, although at a later date I prayed formally with a pastor.

Confession needs to be made for complete forgiveness. The word *confession* means to confess wrongs or mistakes that have been done in the past and acknowledge the guilt that comes with these thoughts and actions in order to make a person clean and clear the conscience. The truth is we were all born into a sinful nature, going all the way back to the Garden of Eden with Adam and Eve.

How big is my God? When I met God in a moment of crisis on that fateful summer night, my God was gigantic and still is today. I still call on Him multiple times throughout my day and not just in moments of crisis. I'm thankful that He loves me and cares for me throughout the issues of my day.

## The Sinner's Prayer: The Story of Unconditional Love

The Story of King David and Bathsheba, 2 Samuel 11, NIV

> 1 In the spring, at the time when kings go off to war, David sent Joab out with the king's men and the whole Israelite army. They destroyed the Ammonites and besieged Rabbah. But David remained in Jerusalem.
>
> 2 One evening David got up from his bed and walked around the roof of the palace. From the roof he saw a woman bathing. The woman was very beautiful, 3 and David sent someone to find out who she was. The man said, "She is Bathsheba, the

daughter of Eliam and the wife of Uriah the Hittite." 4 Then David sent messengers to get her. She came to him, and he slept with her. (Now she was purifying herself from her monthly uncleanness.) Then she went back home. 5 The woman conceived and sent word to David, saying, "I am pregnant."

6 So David sent word to Joab: "Send me Uriah the Hittite," And Joab sent him to David. 7 When Uriah came to him, David asked him how Joab was, how the soldiers were and how the war was going. 8 Then David said to Uriah, "Go down to your house and wash your feet." So Uriah left the palace, and a gift from the king was sent after him.

9 But Uriah slept at the entrance to the palace with all his masters servants and did not go to his house.

10 David was told, "Uriah did not go home." So he asked Uriah, "Haven't you just come home from a military campaign? Why didn't you go home?"

11 Uriah said to David, "The ark and Israel and Judah are staying in tents, and my commander Joab and my lord's men are camped in the open country. How could I go to my house to eat and drink and make love to my wife? As surely as you live, I will not do such a thing!"

12 Then David said to him, "Stay here one more day, and tomorrow I will send you back." So Uriah remained in Jerusalem that day and the next. 13 At David's invitation, he ate and drank with him, and David made him drunk. But in the evening Uriah went out to sleep on his mat among his master's servants; he did not go home.

14 In the morning David wrote a letter to Joab and sent it with Uriah. 15 In it he wrote, "Put Uriah out in the front where the fighting is the fiercest. Then withdraw from him so he will be struck down and die."

16 So while Joab had the city under siege, he put Uriah at a place. Where he knew the strongest defenders were. 17 When the men of the city came out and fought against Joab, some of the men in David's army fell; moreover, Uriah the Hittite died. 18 Joab sent David a full account of the battle.

19 He instructed the messenger: When you have finished giving the king this account of the battle, 20 the king's anger may flare up, and he may ask you, "Why did you get so close to the city to fight? Didn't you know they would shoot arrows from the wall? 21 Who killed Abimelech son of Jerub-Besheth? Didn't a woman drop an upper millstone on him from the wall, so that he died in Thebez? Why did you get so close to the wall?" If he asks you this, then

say to him, "Moreover, your servant Uriah the Hittite is dead."

22 The messenger set out, and when he arrived he told David everything Joab had sent him to say. 23 The messenger said to David, "The men overpowered us and came out against us in the open, but we drove them back to the entrance to the city gate. 24 Then the archers shot arrows at your servants from the wall, and some of the king's men died. Moreover, your servant Uriah the Hittite is dead."

25 David told the messenger, "Say this to Joab: 'Don't let this upset you; the sword devours one as well as another. Press the attack against the city and destroy it.' Say this to encourage Joab."

26 When Uriah's wife heard that her husband was dead, she mourned for him. 27 After the time of mourning was over, David had her brought to his house, and she became his wife and bore him a son. But the thing David had done displeased the Lord.

Recounted in the above paragraphs from the Bible is King David's story. Many times I have heard people say, "I could never be forgiven because of all the things I have done. If God only knew." God does know of everything in our past—the mistakes, the indecisions, the wrongs we have done, and the wrongs committed against you. He knows the hurts, the loneliness and the heartache you have been through.

But let's look through the above scriptures in 2 Samuel 11. King David went to a rooftop viewing area to watch a naked woman take her bath. King David made an arrangement to meet this married woman (Bathsheba) and to have sexual relations with her. Bathsheba became pregnant with King David's baby, while Bathsheba's husband Uriah was fighting in a war. When King David could not trick Uriah into believing the conceived child was his own, he had Uriah sent to the front lines of the battlefield where he was killed in battle.

After all of the previous wrongs of lust, adultery, and deception, David committed murder! Sometime later David asked God for forgiveness and God graciously granted it. Throughout the Bible, King David is known as a man after God's own heart. How incredible is that! If God responds to David with forgiveness for his sins, God can forgive you and me for anything in our past.

A person can never do enough good to make oneself right with God because sin a part of our very nature. We are saved by the forgiveness of sins and only the forgiveness of sins. We cannot enter the kingdom of heaven any other way, only through surrendering your life to Jesus Christ.

We can live a good life, and be good to others but the truth is, we still need forgiveness. The hope and desire is to believe that God can make all things new, and He can. There is freedom in God—freedom from the past and freedom from the hurts of this life. All we need to do is confess our sins, ask forgiveness with our mouths and believe with our hearts that Jesus Christ is our Lord and Savior.

2 Thessalonians 2:13, NETB — "But we ought to thank God always for you, brothers and sisters loved by the Lord, because God chose you from the beginning for salvation through sanctification by the Spirit and faith in the truth."

God created you; He knew you before you were born. God has chosen you as His own. You are unique, and you are loved by the King of Kings and the Lord of Lords.

Luke 12:7, NIV — "Indeed, the very hairs of your head are all numbered. Don't be afraid..."

He even knows the number of hairs on your head. God the Father, Jesus the Son, and the Holy Spirit desire to have a relationship with you, a daily moment-by-moment relationship. It's not about religion but relationship, a moment-by-moment walk with the Creator of the earth for the rest of your life.

Religious traditions are as old as the world itself. History is and will always be important and needs to be remembered, but the heart of the matter is in the redeeming value and relationship with Jesus Christ. Nothing more, nothing less. It's so simple to believe and wonderful to see all He has for you.

> The day will come when every knee will bow and every tongue confess that Jesus Christ is Lord.

Imagine saying each day, "God, this is your day, I surrender it to you. Take it and make it what you would want it to be. Not my will but your will be done. Guide my steps today, lead me where you would have me to go, what you would have me do, and say what you would have me to say." That's total surrender of your will to His. The mere thought removes the burden of the weight you're carrying by giving it to Him. That in itself is freedom in Christ.

Life is hard. Due to the circumstances of the past, we have carried hurts and burdens far too long. Today is the day of freedom when you give those hurts to Him. Turn everything over to Him and make today the day of salvation.

> John 14:6, NASB – "Jesus said to him, 'I am the way, and the truth, and the life; no one comes to the Father but through Me.'"

The prayer of salvation and freedom is the prayer of letting go of the years and the memories that have tormented you and surrendering your heart with the kingship of the Lord Jesus. You can be made new right now in the eyes of the Lord. Today you can be born again; today you can start life over again. Today your past can be gone, and you can have a fresh beginning.

My friend Todd wrote this example on how to come to the loving forgiveness of our Lord Jesus Christ shortly before he died. Todd was an amazing friend. He lived his life on purpose, living out his faith in every area of his life.

God is Holy (pure, without sin).

God is Love (wants all to know Him).

God is Just (sin must be punished).

We all have rebelled against God.

Even one sin is enough to separate us from God.

God's requirement is for us to be perfect.

This happens through Christ!

Admit you're a sinner.

Be willing to turn from your sin.

Believe Jesus Christ died for you on the cross and rose from the grave.

Through prayer, invite Jesus Christ to be the Savior and leader of your life.

Praying Repentance:

Repent of the sin: call it what it is; it is your sin.

Receive God, ask for forgiveness and cleansing.

Rebuke the enemy's hold of you because of the sin.

Replace all lies with God's truth.

The angels in heaven rejoice each time someone prays a prayer of salvation. Salvation is not a matter of family religion, family traditions, or the biblical knowledge you can recite. Salvation is not what's in your head; it's a matter of the heart. Pray this prayer of salvation; pray it out loud and from your heart. Believe this prayer as you say it.

## The Prayer of Salvation:

Heavenly Father,

Thank you for loving me. I repent of my sins, ask for forgiveness, and open my heart to Jesus to come and live inside of me.

Jesus, you are my Lord and Savior. I believe you died for my sins and you were raised from the dead so that I may have eternal life.

Thank you Father for forgiving me. Today I am a new person in Christ and on my way to Heaven.

Thank you for saving me.

Amen

After praying the prayer of salvation, you are a new person and a member of God's family. Find a Bible-believing church and attend regularly, worshipping and learning with others about your new walk in Christ. Find at least one strong mentor in the Christian faith to help you grow and be all that you can be in the body of Christ.

## CHAPTER 15 DISCUSSION QUESTIONS

### LIFE LESSONS

The story of King David's life sums it up for a lot of people. Some people feel they cannot be forgiven because they had made wrong or poor choices in their life. After King David's repentance, God said David is a man after my own heart. Through our mistakes God loves us and calls each of us into repentance and forgiveness of our sins.

## Points to Ponder

The Bible says God is omnipresent, which means He is everywhere and knows all things, everything that you and I have done. Have you ever felt you couldn't be forgiven for something you have done?

It's been said, "It was a God thing." Explain a time when God has really showed up right when you needed Him most.

The power of forgiveness is about forgiving the wrongs from your past. Have you asked God to forgive your sins, and do you know that your heart is right with Him?

# CHAPTER 16

# Prayer Has Eternal Blessings

Ecclesiastes 3:11, NIV—"He has made everything beautiful in its time. He has also set eternity in the human heart; yet no one can fathom what God has done from beginning to end."

*Hearing the voice of their Holy Spirit, then speaking the truth in gentleness and respect has eternal blessings.*

S ome years ago on a very cold Michigan winter evening God spoke to my heart. Living in Michigan my entire life, I have seen some of the worst winter weather on the planet. One particular night around 7:00 PM. the outside temperature was already below zero, and the wind chill temperatures were twenty-five below with near white-out conditions of blowing snow.

While watching television I felt God speak to me about visiting my great-uncle Harry who was dying of cancer in the hospital. A thought raced through my mind: *No one would venture out on these horrible roads even to make a hospital visit.* Not wanting to go out in such weather, I reasoned that I would do it another time.

But the feeling kept coming over me again and again. So I got out of my chair and dressed to go. Visiting hours ended at 8:00 PM, and it was now ten after seven. I figured with the bad roads I could just make it before close of visiting hours. I carefully drove my car down the highway at only twenty-five miles an hour. The blowing snow made the lane look more like a two-track trail through the woods. But even the hazardous road conditions couldn't keep my mind off what God was speaking to my heart.

You see, back then I was uncomfortable walking into a hospital room to talk and pray with anyone. I was new in my faith, and I lacked confidence in myself to do what might be considered a pastor's job. Yet the closer I got to the hospital, the stronger I felt the need to pray with Uncle Harry.

When you hear the voice of the Holy Spirit, you know it. When you act on what the Holy Spirit says, you now realize you are no longer a bench player. God has called you up from the minor leagues to take action. I heard the voice of the Holy Spirit and stepped forth in obedience somewhere between faith and "I think I can do this."

I had only seen Uncle Harry a number of times in my life. He was far from a stranger, as he would come over for Thanksgiving and Christmas meals, but we had little in common for any kind of real conversation. He was a quiet older man who had lost his wife many years before. It was kind of my mother to think of him so he could be with family. Soon the reality hit me that I didn't know him very well and that this visit might be quite awkward. My mind began to wrestle back and forth between courage and fear.

> Ephesians 6:19, ESV — "…and also for me, that words may be given to me in opening my mouth boldly to proclaim the mystery of the gospel…"

I remembered the truth that if God sends you, He will enable you to do it. So I prayed as I got closer to the hospital, *God give me the words to speak….help me to convey your message….open Uncle Harry's heart to what you would have me say.*

Again the human nature side of fear objected, *This visit wasn't about how well the Tigers might do or the off-season trades the team made. It was about sharing Jesus with a man dying in the natural, a difficult conversation for me to begin with!* More fear crept into my mind. *What if he flat out rejected me and my visit?* The insecure fears from childhood came welling up inside of me, like when I was delivering newspapers to the boys' home and being chased by the German Shepherd dog named Jackie. I heard the voice of my oldest brother Steve, the paper route boss, saying *Get going; you can do it!*

I pulled into the hospital ramp and parked my car. One moment I felt confident I was doing the right thing by walking in obedience as God was directing my steps. Then when I walked down the hall nearing his room, my emotions changed to uncertainty about what might happen. I looked at the clock on the wall, and it was 7:50 PM, ten minutes left of visiting hours.

Uncle Harry was nearing death as the cancer had taken over his body. I walked into the room and was greeted by his nurse. She said you have just a couple of minutes before you will have to leave. I said I just came to pray with him, and she said ok. The nurse was writing some notes as I walked up to the hospital bed.

> Colossians 1:14, NIV—"…in whom we have redemption, the forgiveness of sins."

---

Hearing the voice of their Holy Spirit, then speaking the truth in gentleness and respect has eternal blessings.

---

I said, "Hello, Uncle Harry." As he slowly opened his eyes, I shared a short story about God's love, and asked him if he would like to pray a prayer of salvation and ask Jesus into his heart; he nodded yes. I put one hand on his head and held his hand with the other, and we prayed together. All my fears went away; it was like a love story between Uncle Harry and God. We finished praying and said Amen together. He looked happy as I turned to leave.

As I walked toward the door I said good night to the nurse. I heard the beep-beep-beep of the heart monitor that would soon became a flat line, and she ran to his bedside and then called for the doctors. After I had exited the room, Uncle Harry met Jesus face to face at that moment. The nurse had tears in her eyes as she had just witnessed a miracle. Uncle Harry had accepted Jesus into his heart shortly before he passed away. God's timing is amazing; He is always on time every time.

The story of Uncle Harry is a story of God's faithfulness of how much He cares and loves each and every one of us. That time God chose to use me as a messenger of the good news to fulfill His will and promise of love for Uncle Harry. Still, many years later, I think back that the God of the universe chose me to share the good news about salvation. I had no previous knowledge of Uncle Harry's religious views or any background of his beliefs or his faith.

When you hear the voice of the Holy Spirit you move in faith, because eternity might hang in the balance for someone, and you may be the person God calls to share your faith.

The power of forgiveness opened the doors to the power of prayer, which allowed my close and personal relationship with the God of the universe. Because of that relationship, I live my life on purpose, to love and serve others.

Like Uncle Harry, every one of us needs forgiveness in our lives. Make today the day of salvation making Jesus the Lord of your life. Like Uncle Harry, we are all sinners saved by grace.

## CHAPTER 16 DISCUSSION QUESTIONS

---

### LIFE LESSONS

A life that can change can be used by God to help others. If we are open to be used God will use us. Many times in my life God has spoken to me about doing this or saying that only to see that I was the person chosen to lead someone to Christ, an eternal change in someone's destiny.

---

## Points to Ponder

Most people are nervous about sharing their faith; they might lack confidence or may be afraid of rejection if they speak out. Has God ever spoken to you to go and talk to someone about your faith?

We people are the church; what do you do to share your faith?

Have you ever led someone to the Lord? What did the experience feel like to be used by the God of the universe to change the course of eternity for someone?

# CHAPTER 17

# The Power of Prayer

James 5:16, NIV — "...The prayer of a righteous person is powerful and effective."

*The depth of your prayer life reflects the depth of your relationship in Christ.*

*Go deep, go deeper than before; empty yourself before Him.*

I met Jesus in the heat of the moment back when I was sixteen years old. In the days before the robbery, I didn't do a whole lot of praying, except for a few routine prayers my parents taught us as small children. You may remember the typical meal prayer that went something like this: "God is great, God is good, let us thank Him for our food. Amen." Or the old bedtime standby: "Now I lay me down to sleep, I pray the Lord my soul to keep." Nothing wrong with either of those prayers because at first people do not know how to pray or how to begin their personal journey with Jesus Christ. However, as we grow in our Christian walk, so should our prayer life.

It would be hard to imagine praying childlike prayers as an adult where nothing is personal, but rather totally routine and prayed out of tradition rather than from the heart. Our prayer life should grow as we get to know God better. Prayers from the heart sound more like an affectionate conversation with your best friend. Prayer is not a wish list of my wants and desires, but prayer is like a respectful exchange of love, thankfulness, submission, and obedience to God Almighty.

Our God is a big and amazing God who desires a close and personal relationship with each and every one of us. So if we can think past religious traditions and move toward an intimate moment-by-moment relationship with God the Father, Jesus the Son, and the Holy Spirit, our spiritual walk with Jesus Christ becomes personal. God is always there waiting for us and wants us to know Him in a deep personal way, but it takes effort on our part to seek Him out.

After my robbery event, I began to read and try to understand the Bible by reading small segments each night before going to bed. Honestly, I read very small amounts and tried to find the meanings of scripture and apply it to my everyday life. So early on I was not going to be a person who would read through the Bible in a year. I ingested just small bits of truth to ponder and add some substance to my new walk with Christ.

After my nightly reading, I would pray to God and thank Him for my day, ask Him to care of my family, and to keep me safe as I slept. As time went on, my prayers went deeper and deeper. I began to trust God with my more of my life, to understand that He is in control and that I trust Him with everything I have. I began to understand forgiveness. My faith became more about trusting Him, and my walk became bolder as the days and months past.

I believe the power of prayer opened the dialog between me and God, which opened the door to the power of forgiveness in my life. And forgiveness opened the door to where my life is today. If I had held onto anger and bitterness toward the grocery store robbers, my life would be totally different. Forgiveness enables me to no longer dwell on insecurities caused by the robbery. The healing that forgiveness provides has value beyond measured results, and the intrinsic rewards cannot be put into words.

In all areas of my life I have always wanted to reach my potential, and my faith walk would be no different. One day I would want God to use me to share my faith with others and use my life as a witness to the gospel. Forgiveness and prayer made that possible.

I own a construction a company that is located in the Midwest. Every Monday morning I would leave my home in Michigan to travel to Wisconsin or Minnesota, which required passing through Chicago. To beat the heavy Chicago traffic, I needed to leave my home between three and four in the morning. If I waited any later I would be stuck in traffic jams for hours, which would be frustrating and a complete waste of my time.

Many hours of driving can get boring really fast! So to pass the time more quickly I listened to countless hours of news, financial reports, sports, and every kind of music on the radio. After that I would still get bored out of my mind, so I started channel surfing trying to find anything that would stimulate my mind and make the miles go by faster. On some occasions, I even listened to various books on tape to fill my mind with learning and to inspire creative thinking.

As I left my house one Monday morning, I decided to try something different. I began to pray. No radio distractions, just quiet time between me and God as I drive through the darkness. There are hundreds of things to pray for, such as family members, life situations, God's will for my life, my kids, our government, my employees, and countless other things. At first my Monday morning prayer times would last an hour, then an hour and a half, and sometimes as long as three hours. My time was well spent as I prayed and sang praise songs in worship. And I found the miles went by much faster than before.

I was able to turn unproductive drive time into one of the most productive personal prayer times in my life. It was during these times of praying for other people that my heart began to change. My thoughts centered on God as I asked Him to inspire me with creative thoughts in all areas of my life. I believe my life today is a reflection of those early morning prayer times as I drove across the country.

> 2 Timothy 1:14, NIV – "...the Holy Spirit who lives in us."

---

The depth of your prayer life reflects the depth of your relationship in Christ.

Go deep, go deeper than before; empty yourself before Him.

---

Prayer time is personal; it's amazingly personal to me. The closeness in my prayer life with God the Father, Jesus the Son, and the Holy Spirit has completely changed my life. The ability to hear the voice of the Holy Spirit helps me to move forward as the Spirit directs me. I know His voice when He speaks to me. Sometimes He directs me to pray for a person who is sick, a complete stranger in a grocery store, or a person walking on the street.

As my prayer times grew, so did the dreams God put in my heart. I have asked God to use me or to help others. Imagine waking up each morning and saying, "Lord this is your day. I give it to you, not my will but your will be done. Lead me in my thoughts, and my actions today. Help me in my meetings and my interactions with others. May my focus today be to put others first before me." These are life-changing, game-changing statements to pray to God the Father, Jesus the Son, and the Holy Spirit. When you do, amazing things will begin to happen, and your life will begin to change.

The power of prayer has led to many opportunities for me to step out in faith and help others. I listen for the voice of the Holy Spirit as I look for opportunity to serve others. One morning I was going to a meeting in downtown Grand Rapids. I pulled up to a parking meter and struggled to find the correct change for the meter.

After some delay, the meter was set for forty minutes. I walked into my meeting, which lasted for only three or four minutes, and I walked back out to my truck. I looked up the street and saw a coffee shop a block and a half away. I put my meeting items back in the truck and headed up the street to get a coffee.

As I neared the coffee shop a homeless man walked up to me and asked for some spare change. He said, "Sir, could you spare some change so I can get something to eat?" My response was, "No sir, I will not give you any money that could be used for drugs or alcohol." He replied, "Thank you, God bless you anyway sir." I turned and said, "I will walk you into a nearby breakfast shop and buy you a breakfast, anything you want."

A great big smile spread across his face. As he ordered his meal he asked, "Can I order a large glass of milk?" I replied, "Of course." I paid for the meal and told him I would be back in a few minutes to talk. He made himself comfortable in a booth while his food was being prepared. Back at my truck I grabbed a daily devotional from inside and returned to the restaurant. He was just starting to eat, so I sat next to him and showed him how the devotional was meant to be read each day. After explaining how the book could help him, we talked about God and how much God loves him.

Was this event just a mere coincidence or perhaps a chance meeting on the street, or was it an opportune moment directed by the Holy Spirit? This is an example of how God used me to help out another person, showing him love, respect, and kindness. I hope he is doing well today. In my life the power of forgiveness has allowed me to grow in the Lord, which has made the power of prayer between me and the Father closer than I could have ever imagined.

Another time while working in a small inner city church I heard the voice of the Holy Spirit. The empty church had been boarded up for about twenty-five years, and dirt and filth covered everything. As I was walking through the lower level kitchen, I saw an old stove. Looking past the peeling paint I asked the pastor if the stove worked. He replied, "No, it's not up to code and cannot be used."

I looked it over and measured the size of the space it was fit into. I asked the pastor if we replaced the stove would the church be able to serve meals to the inner city neighborhood residents? He answered, "Absolutely yes — we would!"

I began to pray about it, and the more I prayed the more passion I had for the project. So I researched the cost of a new stove and found the project would run about $4,500. With the help of my Tuesday morning men's group, we quickly raised about $3,000 cash! The pastors of the church also did some fundraising and the balance was made up from a couple of businessmen. The stove was ordered, and the day came to install it. After some adjustments, the new ten burner double oven stove was hooked up and ready to be used.

The church ladies began cooking meals, and the newcomers came to hear a gospel message and enjoy a meal afterward. After twenty months over 6,300 meals have been served and the meals program is going strong. The meals serve a wonderful purpose of feeding hungry people; that in itself is well worth the effort.

God sees the long-term effects beyond the meals program. The act of feeding people can lead to life-changing decisions in people's lives for themselves, for their children, and for generations yet to come. The church ladies' lives have also been changed because someone was praying for them long ago.

It is through the power of prayer that a family tree begins to change; it begins to bend a little more in a new direction where the families now see an eternal hope for their future, and through this church people are loved just the way they are, and so the prayers are answered as the love comes down from the Father once again through His people to serve those in need.

The power of prayer through the meals program is an amazing ministry in itself. As the church ladies cook, they pray for the house to be full and that hearts will be open to hearing God's word. As the people come in the doors to receive, the ladies continue to pray, and as they serve the food they continue to pray.

God the Father has heard the prayers of His people. During the short time the meals have been served, approximately 625 people have prayed a prayer of forgiveness and received salvation for their sins. Asking God to use us will always have eternal rewards.

## CHAPTER 17 DISCUSSION QUESTIONS

> ### LIFE LESSONS
>
> The power of prayer is amazing in my life. God has used my prayer life to benefit others. God desires to have a close and intimate relationship with his people. The power of prayer is personal between you and God.

Points to Ponder

Many times our prayer life can be routinely filled with a wish list of our wants and needs. Do you pray out of routine, and tradition or is it more personal?

In what ways has your prayer life changed your life?

Write down times when your prayer is so personal, so powerful and God moved...

# CHAPTER 18

# The Journey of Hurts, Pain, and Forgiveness

> Revelation 21:4, NIV — "He will wipe away every tear from their eyes. There will be no more death or mourning or crying or pain, for the order of things has passed away..."

*May His peace and comfort be with those who hurt deeply.*

Our destiny is born out of the hardest moments in life; we are delivered out of the most difficult times. Working through the hardest moments of your life, the uphill climb to be the person with a story to tell and the person God has called you to be is never easy and never ending. The journey is always difficult to endure. There is always joy in the morning, and your story is to tell of God's faithfulness, and your testimony is to share with others, to proclaim the power of God in your life. Therefore I declare I am an overcomer in Jesus' name.

I needed to conquer fear head on if I was going to make something of my life. Life gives you thousands of opportunities behind a closed door. Opening the door and walking through into the unknown presents wonderful opportunities and adventures. Standing at the door and not opening it allows fear to determine your future and perhaps a life unlived to its potential. For me, I needed to walk through the door facing fear one step at a time to enjoy my life and future God had in store for me.

Life is about taking risks. Injured people sometimes hesitate here; there is an unnatural hesitation to step back to access and reevaluate before moving forward. What's going to win: the fear of the past or the promise of your future?

Being called out trying to steal second base in little league baseball game as a kid results in fear the next time he is put into a clutch situation again that he could fail and be called out again. Then later in life as an adult, we must overcome adolescent fears and embarrassment of our youthful mistakes to live up to our God-given potential.

Held back by fear to never try again would be like living the robbery over and over and over again, allowing it to take over and have complete control of my life. Life is an experience and quite unfair at times, but how we deal with the unfairness of the past determines our future.

My brother and I along with our friend Mark found this farm quite by accident one day after school when I was fifteen years old. We had read in an outdoor magazine that whitetail deer hunting was very good outside of town. So we decided to pack our hunting gear, and after school, we would drive to the area the magazine described and knock on some doors and ask for permission to hunt on someone's farm.

After school we had about two hours before the darkness would start to settle in. *What a life,* I thought as we grabbed our gear and headed for the country. As we drove down the highway we saw a highway sign for Newaygo. It sounded good, so we exited the highway and drove through town. The three of us scanned the countryside making comments like that place looks good and the next area looked better than the previous spot, and so on.

I was the youngest in the group, usually with a lot to say. When I looked at one farm I said, *That's the place; stop the car, and I will ask for permission for us to bow hunt.* I walked up to the front door knocked and an elderly man and woman came to the door. I introduced myself and asked for permission to hunt. They were a nice friendly couple and they said go ahead young man, enjoy yourself.

It's a beautiful eighty-acre piece in the heart of Michigan farm country. It has two ponds, a small creek with a pasture, high rolling wooded hills, and a swamp full of cattails and frogs. The farm is full of wildlife: beautiful whitetail deer, ducks, owls, rabbits, fox, and pheasants. It has winding trail system that accesses all areas of the farm, perfect for nature walks and hiking.

That afternoon started a nice friendship that lasted almost forty years; the couple has since passed away. My brother and I own that farm today and we have had a lifetime of making memories on that land. My brother and I brought our children out there as babies, and today our grandchildren are enjoying wonderful hikes through the woods, helping with planting food plots and a pumpkin patch where we pick pumpkins in the fall.

Through the years we have hunted, camped, worked the land, and fished in the two ponds that are full of blue-gills and bass. As we have become older men, we take off Wednesday afternoons to plow fields and work food plots.

Each fall we invite families to come out and take hay-rides with their children and pick pumpkins to enjoy each October. The farm has provided wonderful family times that we can provide free of charge to friends and family. Just simple family fun. After the wagon rides we make a campfire where kids roast hot dogs and marshmallows and enjoy cider and doughnuts.

The farmer, whose name was James, was a hardworking man. He was a child of the depression, and his family understood hard times. He grew up in northern Michigan on a small farm; his father worked various jobs to make ends meet. Outhouse toilets were the normal way life along with hand-me-down clothing. About half of small town kids quit high school and left home to join the service; James joined the Navy and proudly served his country.

After his military service time, James headed to the big city to work in one of the appliance manufacturing fac-tories on an assembly line. Later he worked in the main-tenance department repairing the assembly lines and machines. Sometime around 1950, James purchased his farm in Newaygo County. James was a tough man. You could understand that from his language—his statements were often filled with a mix of swear words. Over time I have tried not to judge people by their language or actions; they are just outward examples of pain and frustrations coming out in their life through their language.

> 2 Corinthians 7:10, NET — "For sadness as intended by God produces a repentance that leads to salvation, leaving no regret, but worldly sadness brings about death."

Some people you meet in life speak crudely from their culture or maybe from the environment in which they were raised. Others perhaps speak in a way that their language is spoken as an outpouring of personal pain and hardship. I believe that was James' way.

It was easy to see James had good manners, and though his clothing would be out of style, he did his best to dress up if going out for dinner or to one of our homes for a holiday meal. I think James was raised in a loving home, although he was never spoiled.

The look in his James' eyes was full of pain, the kind of pain an older man would have difficulty talking about. He expressed himself mostly by blaming others for their foolish mistakes, and an unmistaken stubborn side of him that could not compromise on any situation; he was right, and that was that.

He was truly an old-school type of guy who would go to any length to fix something and not spend money for a proper repair. Over the years James began to open up about his life by sharing stories from his childhood with my brother and me.

James' dad was an undersheriff in a northern Michigan county, and James would sometimes ride along with his on police calls. One time when James was about ten years old, a call came in over the radio to be on the lookout for two men who just robbed a store. The robbers were soon spotted, and the police chase began. Sometime after a high speed chase, the robbers pulled over, and James' dad pulled the guys out of the car. James' dad handed James his service revolver to hold on the robbers while he put them in handcuffs. That's an amazing amount of responsibility for a ten-year-old boy, but all went well and the men were taken to jail.

> May His peace and comfort be with those who hurt deeply.

You never know what someone has gone through in their past. At some time in a particular conversation, James began to open up. My brother and I must have gained his trust over the years helping cut loads of firewood to heat his house in the cold Michigan winters. We would take breaks from the hard work, sit up in the woods, and drink water, and conversations would begin.

James had lost a son to a childhood sickness. I think the boy was seven or eight years old and developed some rare form of kidney disease. There were a lot of hospital stays, but eventually the illness overtook the young boy, and he passed away. As he told the story there were no tears, but he gave you the feeling of being angry at God for his loss.

James continued to talk, this time about another son who son was about twenty-five years old. This son was a jack of all trades, the kind of man who had lots of natural talents. At an early age, he could take car motors apart, rebuild them, and put them back together without any formal training. This son was married and had two daughters. One night while on his motorcycle, he was hit driving through an intersection and was killed instantly. James considered this son reckless, and had he been more careful, he wouldn't have been killed.

Then some years later his granddaughters, now sixteen and twelve, were driving too fast on a country road not far from the farm. There were swerving tire marks left on the asphalt before one of the girls lost control of the car; the car rolled several times, and James' two granddaughters died instantly when they were thrown from the car. The granddaughters were all what was left from their dad who was killed in the motorcycle accident. Losing his two young granddaughters was an exceptionally hard loss for James.

I'm sure the crudeness of his language was in part of the pain due to the losses in his life. The look into his eyes told the stories of hurt and heartache that he was unable to describe with his words until he would shut down the conversation or change the subject due to the inability to talk about it any further.

It was good to sit and listen as he shared those difficult moments in his life. Life has taught me to sit and be quiet and let others talk as they describe their pain of past circumstances. Life is hard, but it's even harder if you are living out these moments on your own without faith. Without faith you reason the whys and how things happened, leaving many unanswered questions. Frustrations lead to anger and bitterness and then onto the hardness of heart, which becomes a prominent trait in your personality.

As the years went by James' health began to decline and when appropriate we talked about God and about heaven. James was a tough cookie to crack. He never responded by wanting to hear more; he just looked and listened, sometimes with statements like heaven is not big enough for everyone, and why does that person get to go while others cannot.

We told him the truth, and we told him in love, although his unique questions were somewhat frustrating at the time. Over time love won out; there were fewer questions, and he would do more listening. The listening led us to pray with him, and ultimately praying a prayer of forgiveness for his salvation. Shortly afterward late on a Friday night, James met Jesus face to face.

Praying a prayer of forgiveness was a forty-year journey for James; there was nothing easy about it as he continued to hurt so deeply from the pain of losing his loved ones. Accepting Jesus into his heart was the beginning of James' healing process. What might have happened had James accepted Christ into his life earlier in his life? I have no idea, but it was God's perfect timing for James' life at that time, nothing more, nothing less.

The pain became a way of life for James. It became his constant companion because the memories of the family losses were almost impossible for James to deal with. If God is God why did my son get sick and die? I miss my granddaughters; why didn't God protect them? No one has the answers to these questions. By faith, we believe God has a better plan and as hard as that is, we must trust God that He has it right.

When James prayed a prayer of forgiveness it was a modern-day miracle. The angels in heaven rejoiced when his forgiveness had taken place. I cannot tell you James' hurts instantly went away, but I can say with certainty the direction for his life changed that very moment.

One of the most amazing things about the farm was leading James to Christ as he prayed a prayer of forgiveness before he passed away. Who could have thought forty years earlier when a fifteen-year-old boy riding in the back seat of a 1970 Ford Fairlane said, *That's the place*, a forty-year friendship would begin and end with eternal implications.

Not by chance or mere coincidence, nothing more or nothing less than God's perfect timing, where the Holy Spirit was at work on a forty-year journey as He developed the relationship between all of us, leading to an eternal decision where the ultimate moment of forgiveness had taken place. One heart made right in the Lord—I'm still amazed at how good our God is that He chose to use my brother and me in the James' life in forgiveness process.

## CHAPTER 18 DISCUSSION QUESTIONS

### Life Lessons

God is in the middle of everything. The journey in this chapter is forty years long. James the farmer had several lifetimes of pain and hardship in his life, he hurt so deeply. Through relationships God put us together and James found Jesus in the end. Sometimes we just need to listen to the pain and hardships of others, and when appropriate speak a word of love.

## Points to Ponder

God is always at work, sometimes for years before something happens. Can you see something in your life that reflects how God is working in your life?

Relationships are the one of the most important keys to life; people best learn in the community of other like-minded believers. Explain how God has used a relationships in your life.

One of the biggest misconceptions people have is they need to be a Bible expert in order to help hurting people. Explain how God has used you to minister someone who hurts deeply.

# CHAPTER 19

# Open Letter to My Robbers

Matthew 6:14-15, NIV — "For if you forgive other people when they sin against you, your heavenly Father will also forgive you. But if you do not forgive others their sins, your Father will not forgive your sins."

*Forgiveness is something you bring before the Father; it's personal between Him and you. When you do, your healing begins.*

As I write this today, it has been exactly forty-two years since my robbery night. The trauma of that night will live with me as long as I live on this earth. From my heart I say to them: I have forgiven you for the hurt and shame that you have caused me; it's important that you know this. It is through my personal relationship with Jesus Christ that I have moved on and laid this at the foot of the cross.

Forgiveness is my final act of caring for someone who has hurt me more deeply than anyone could understand. I care because Christ has called me to do this, nothing more or nothing less. It is through His love that I have trusted Him to share this personal story through painful memories and many sleepless nights.

I believe in my heart that you made some very bad choices that August night, choices that almost cost me my life. By the grace of God, I was saved, not just in my physical life but most importantly in my spiritual life. That night you decided to rob a local grocery store had some amazing consequences for everyone involved. My life, along with Walt's and my co-worker Jim, hung in the balance somewhere between life and death.

I suspect you were high on drugs and not thinking correctly as you thought up the idea and then the plan to rob the store of its cash that night. As you entered the store and you hid in the darkness of the stockroom, my God had another plan, a plan of salvation for me. It's where I met Him in a close and very personal way.

My life was changed that night, although it seemed like an eternity. I spent the next forty-eight minutes of the worst trauma I thought I could endure, but it was the way I met Jesus through the deal I made with Him: get me out of this and I will serve you forever.

Forty-two years later I love Jesus more today than ever before. It is through His love that I understand forgiveness. If I didn't choose to forgive today, I might have become a miserable, angry bitter man. I chose forgiveness and the life and the freedom it provides.

One day I will stand before God the Father and give an account of my life, the good times and the difficult times. How could I answer Him with pain and bitterness, anger and holding resentment in my heart? I cannot, so this is why in the midst of pain, trauma, and nightmares I choose to forgive you. I hold nothing against you. I hold nothing back. I forgive you both forever and ever.

By no means am I happy about going through the moments and wounds of trauma, being in such shock one moment to outright panic the next. Then I was just simply following your made-up moment-by-moment decisions and instructions on what to do with me next. I called out to God and asked Him for another chance and told Him that if He gave this to me I would serve Him all the days of my life. This is and will be the best of my victim's experience. I found Jesus in the heat of the moment, and I have made good on my end of the deal.

My love for Jesus flows deep into my soul; nothing can separate me from the love of my God.

Through it all God has been loving and kind, and my source of peace and comfort in literally thousands of difficult circumstances, and we have shared some amazingly great days as I am a husband, father, and grandfather to my family. Yes, a thousand times yes, my God is so good to me. For the last forty-two years I have been on an incredible faith walk journey, and Jesus has walked with me each and every step of the way.

Still to this day I hate walking into dark spaces, and dislike people walking behind me in just about any circumstance. I never wear a tie around my neck and still several times a year I wake from my night's sleep gasping, dreaming that something sharp is held against my throat.

> Forgiveness is something you bring before the Father; it's personal between Him and you. When you do, your healing begins.

Rest assured I have never liked even talking about this or sharing this story with anyone. Being tied up with a knife pressed against my throat and my hands held behind my back and a knife poking into my lower spine being held against my will. Then to tie my hands behind my back, tie my ankles together while holding the knives against my skin and hopping for about seventy-five hops across the stockroom floor without cutting my head off was a complete miracle of God. The moments were horrible, but the shame I felt of not being able to defend myself against this madness and being caught completely off guard and defenseless was equally as bad.

Submitting to the actions of two crazy people, and doing everything within my power to just stay alive.

My writing about this is freedom for me, complete and amazing freedom for me, and maybe for you. Each and every person has been hurt by somebody in this world. My hope is that as you read this you will find it in your heart to forgive the people that have hurt you. The hurts of this world are deep and personal, and very personal to you.

My sharing this is my effort to see something good come out of my personal tragedy. My prayer is that you can find forgiveness in your heart and that you are able to forgive others that have hurt you.

## A NOTE TO THE READER

As I began to write this book, I tried to find the names of the brothers who robbed the grocery store. After much research I gave up the effort and laid it into God's hands. If we ever meet again I will introduce them to forgiveness and its power and what it's done for me and what it can do for them. How amazing it could be to lead them into a prayer of salvation, leading them into forgiveness. Today this matter is in God's hands, as it has always has been. My life is a work in process, but today is an amazing day, a day of personal freedom for me.

I pray for the brothers who robbed the grocery store that night at 10:12 PM, for the following forty-eight minutes of trauma that night, the night that changed my life. I pray that they find forgiveness in their hearts with our Lord and Savior Jesus Christ, that their lives are made right. My hope is they have learned from their experience and prison time, and are made new in a relationship with Jesus Christ today.

I encourage every reader to examine their hearts from childhood, from abuse, from not being cared for, from absent moms and dads, to unfaithful husbands and wives. To the drunk driver who killed a child or another family member or close friend. To the moms who choose to give up their babies in difficult times or to moms who never knew them at all.

Whether it is the thousands of circumstances of hurts in this world of cruelty toward innocent victims or to the one thing in your heart that still hurts, bring it to the cross, and forgive those who know not what they have done.

Most of all find forgiveness for your sins and make your heart right before God. This is the day of salvation; this is your day, my friend. Unload the thousands of pounds of hurt, guilt, and living your life for yourself. Invite Jesus into your heart today, ask for forgiveness, for He is ready to forgive you no matter what ever you have done. There is no circumstance that can change His love for you, because He loves you so much, just the way you are.

This, my friend, is the power of forgiveness.

## CHAPTER 19 DISCUSSION POINTS

> ### LIFE LESSONS
>
> The ultimate moment of forgiveness is for praying for those who have hurt you, praying that they meet the God the Father, Jesus the Son, and the Holy Spirit of the universe and that their hearts are made right. For me to reach this point completed the healing on my 42-year journey from my robbery night. Look deep within yourselves, you can do this.

## Points to Ponder

Have you come to the place to forgive those that have hurt you, and if not why?

Are you holding on to the past, being held back by unforgiveness issues?

Have you considered writing a letter to those who have hurt you, (even if you have no intention of mailing the letter) as an exercise in expressing deep hurts, regrets or frustrations toward the people that have caused you pain?

As I write, I know one day I will stand before God and give an account of my life. As much as the robbers had hurt me, I chose forgiveness over anger, resentment, and bitterness. If you have been hurt or abused, can you bring these issues before the Father and truly forgive those who have hurt you?

Human beings make mistakes, every one of us. Have you come to the point of forgiving yourself for the mistakes you have made?

The purpose of this book is to show the reader the power of forgiveness and the freedom that it provides. Forgiveness ultimately begins between the reader and God, finding forgiveness for your sins. Are you the reader at peace with God? Why or why not?

# About the Author

Michael was born and raised in Grand Rapids, Michigan area and has lived in Western Michigan his entire life. He is married to his wife Robin, and together they have four children and four grandchildren. Mike and Robin attend Resurrection Life Church in Grandville and also are involved in several other ministries. When not running the general construction company that he and wife Robin and brother Phil own, Mike enjoys spending time with his family, watching his grandchildren play sports, or working the farmland he and his brother share to manage and hunt whitetail deer with family. Mike also enjoys fishing, working in the yard, spending time in his new hobby of painting, and traveling with his wife Robin.

# Your Story

Comments? Please email us at
MSCooleysr@gmail.com.